Recipes from

WHAT'S COOKING

with

RUTH FREMES

Book Five

Recipes from

WHAT'S COOKING

with

RUTH FREMES

Book Five

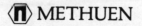 METHUEN

Toronto   New York   London   Sydney   Auckland

Canadian Cataloguing in Publication Data

Fremes, Ruth, 1930–
    Recipes from What's Cooking with Ruth Fremes

Includes index.
ISBN 0-458-94640-0 (v. 1). — ISBN 0-458-95180-3 (v. 2)
ISBN 0-458-95780-1 (v. 3). — ISBN 0-458-97180-4 (v. 4)
ISBN 0-458-98180-X (v. 5)

1. Cookery.   I. What's cooking with Ruth Fremes
(Television program).   II. Title.

TX715.F73 1980   641.5   C80-094824-6

Printed and bound in Canada
1 2 3 4   84   88 87 86 85

Contents

AN OPEN LETTER TO MY VIEWERS

After seven years in the same kitchen, anyone could run out of ideas. Luckily for me, your letters, filled with support and fresh ideas serve as inspiration. Without them, there are times when I would be standing before you with a blank face and an empty table.

Even though there is seldom time for me to communicate with you directly, your letters are read and the ideas you send are always considered; often used. When you said the recipes were read too quickly, I slowed down. When you asked for more low calorie or simple dinner recipes, we tried to react as swiftly as possible. We do pretape "What's Cooking" and so couldn't react directly, but your ideas were incorporated into later programs.

There were many compliments, some brick bats and even some beautiful homemade gifts. To all who took time to write to me, thank you. Some viewers share my sense of humor and sent ideas and recipes that we agreed were absurd. We even have a file marked *Recipes We Never Finished Reading*. Happily, few recipes found their way into this file. Most were wonderful, and for these, I thank you. The folks who work in Studio Seven are a happy group, we enjoy the opportunity of sharing so many hours with you.

Good Health and good wishes to you.

Cordially,

Ruth Fremes
June 1984

APPETIZERS AND SOUPS

Antipasto Giardino

A North Bay viewer once requested a recipe for antipasto. Some time has passed but we found one we liked in our local newspaper! We've renamed it Antipasto Giardino—antipasto from the garden. Antipasto is served before the meal—it's the Italian version of hors d'oeuvres. (Makes 6 pints)

Ingredients

¾ cup vegetable oil

½ small head cauliflower, broken into flowerets

1 large or 2 small green peppers, diced

½ pound (250 g) fresh button mushrooms

1 cup finely sliced carrots

1 cup finely sliced celery

1 13.2-ounce (375 mL) jar sweet pickled onions

2 cups dry white wine

1 cup cider vinegar

4 cloves garlic, crushed

1 bay leaf

1 5½-ounce (156 mL) can tomato paste

Salt, pepper to taste

2 6½-ounce (184 g) cans white tuna chunks (not flakes)

½ cup dill pickles, sliced lengthwise

¾ cup sliced olives with pimento, drained

Method

Heat oil in a large skillet. Add raw vegetables and pickled onion and mix well. Cover and simmer gently for 5 minutes.

Stir in wine, vinegar, garlic and bay leaf and simmer gently, uncovered, until liquid is reduced by about one-third (about 10 minutes). Add tomato paste and simmer a further 10 minutes, then season to taste. Remove from heat to avoid overcooking the vegetables which should still be slightly crisp. Remove bay leaf. Fold in tuna, pickles and olives. Bring to a boil. Taste and adjust for seasoning.

Turn into a large bowl to cool, then spoon into clean jars. Cover and refrigerate. Serve with garlic bread, crackers, melba toast or vegetable sticks.

Sicilian Meatballs with Marinara Sauce

Carlo Middione opened his Italian take-out café, Vivande Porta Via, in San Francisco several years ago, serving ancient recipes from the south of Italy. This is a traditional Sicilian recipe. The mixture of fruit, cinnamon, and pine nuts with the meat is unusual and reflects the Saracen influence in Sicily centuries ago. Originally this dish was made with lean pork rather than veal. (Makes approximately 40 meatballs)

Ingredients

1½	pounds (750 g) veal, finely ground	⅓	cup fine breadcrumbs
2	whole eggs	⅓	cup raisins, white, dark, or mixed
	Zest of 1 lemon, finely grated	½	cup wine vinegar
4	tablespoons roasted pine nuts	1½	teaspoons table salt
2	Amaretti cookies, crumbled	½	teaspoon black pepper
¼	cup whole milk	1	cup Marinara Sauce (following)
¼	teaspoon cinnamon		

Method

Place all ingredients except marinara sauce in a large bowl and mix until well blended. (You can use a mixer on slow speed to do this.) Roll into small meatballs approximately 1¼ inches in diameter.

Roast at 375°F (190°C), shaking the pan often to keep the color even. Test after 10–15 minutes; the meatballs should not be pink in the centre. Remove from oven. The meatballs can be set aside at this point and re-heated before serving. Be sure to cover the meatballs when warming them so they don't dry out.

When ready to serve, heat the marinara sauce and toss the meatballs in it *just to coat*. Serve hot as an appetizer or on a buffet table.

Marinara Sauce

This tart, fresh-tasting tomato sauce is excellent with pasta or as a dipping sauce for Carlo's Sicilian Meatballs. When fresh tomatoes and basil are in season, use them!

Ingredients

1	large yellow onion, finely chopped	1	sprig fresh oregano or 1½ teaspoons dried
¼	cup olive oil	4	leaves fresh basil or 1½ teaspoons dried
2	medium cloves garlic, finely chopped		Salt, pepper to taste
2	8-ounce (226 mL) cans San Marzano tomatoes, finely chopped		Pinch of crushed red pepper (optional)

Method

Put the chopped onion in a wide, heavy pan and add the olive oil. Cook the onions until transparent then add the garlic. Cook about 3 minutes more. Add all the other ingredients and cook at high temperature about 15 minutes, stirring occasionally. The fast cooking will help to reduce the sauce and make it thick, but be careful that it does not burn on the bottom. (The optional pinch of crushed red pepper may be added if a sharper taste is desired.)

Herbed Jerusalem Artichoke Appetizer

Jerusalem artichoke, the vegetable that was discovered in Canada and exported to Europe by Samuel Champlain, is as versatile and homely as the potato. It tastes more like a mild radish than either the potato or artichoke, but blends well with other vegetables. To prepare Jerusalem artichokes, scrub them with a stiff brush under running water. If they are not too knobby, peel before cooking; if knobby, boil for 10 minutes and then peel. Here they are served in a colorful buffet salad. (Serves 8)

Ingredients

¾	pound (400 g) Jerusalem artichokes, scrubbed	3	tablespoons olive oil
1	teaspoon lemon juice	2	tablespoons cider vinegar
½	teaspoon salt	2-3	drops Tabasco sauce
7	small tomatoes, peeled, and finely chopped	¼	cup chopped fresh parsley
3	tablespoons minced green onion	¼	teaspoon marjoram
2	tablespoons finely chopped green pepper		Freshly ground white pepper
			Romaine leaves, rinsed, dried

Method

Place artichokes in a stainless steel or enamel-lined heavy saucepan with enough cold water to cover. Add the lemon juice and salt; heat over medium heat to boiling. Reduce heat to low and cook, covered, until artichokes are crisp-tender, 10–15 minutes. Drain in colander; remove and discard skins. Chop artichokes finely.

Combine the artichokes, tomatoes, green onion and green pepper in a medium-sized bowl. Add the oil, vinegar, and Tabasco sauce, and mix well. Stir in parsley, marjoram and pepper to taste. Place in refrigerator, cover and leave overnight.

To serve, arrange lettuce leaves on a large serving platter. Place artichoke mixture on top.

Hot Garlic-Cheese Bread

Here is the prize-winning recipe, Mahony's Bruschetta, from the 1983 Garlic Festival held in Gilroy, California. It's a hearty first course, wonderful served at a barbecue party. (Serves 6)

Ingredients

1	loaf French or Italian bread without seeds (day-old bread works fine)	½	cup grated hard Romano cheese
10	large cloves fresh garlic, peeled	½	cup grated Parmesan cheese
¾	cup olive oil	3	tablespoons butter
1½	cups 35% cream	1	tablespoon chopped parsley
			paprika

Method

Preheat oven to 350°F (180°C). Cut bread diagonally in one-inch slices, without cutting through bottom crust. In food processor or blender, mince garlic with steel blade and add olive oil with processor running to make a thin paste.

Slather garlic paste on cut surfaces and on top and side crusts of bread. Place directly on rack (with pan on shelf below to catch drippings), and bake for 10–12 minutes, until top is crispy looking. While bread is in oven, heat whipping cream in heavy saucepan. Do not boil. Stir in cheese slowly so that sauce is absolutely smooth (a wire whip works well for this). Stir in butter and keep sauce warm until bread is ready. Wait until everyone is seated at the table. Then place crispy bread in a warmed, shallow serving dish with sides. Finish cutting through bottom crust and pour sauce over. Sprinkle with parsley and paprika and serve immediately. This dish cools very quickly.

Note: Each guest should be provided with a small saucer for the Bruschetta, as it is best eaten with a knife and fork.

Mushrooms In Parchment

(Serves 2)

Ingredients

½	pound fresh plump mushrooms	2	tablespoons breadcrumbs
4	anchovy fillets finely chopped	2	tablespoons olive oil
2	heaping tablespoons finely chopped flat-leafed parsley		Juice of ½ lemon
	Ground black pepper	2	thin slices of lemon for garnish
1	large clove garlic, finely chopped		Parchment paper or brown paper bag

Method

Brush mushrooms to clean them, do not wash unless really necessary. Cut into thin slices and place in a bowl. Add all the other ingredients except the lemon slices. Mix well with your hands or with a fork. Brush paper with oil and place mixture on paper. Place two lemon slices on the mixture. If you use brown paper, oil it first. Seal edges very well by making many overlapping little folds. Brush outside of paper all over with oil and place on baking sheet.

Bake for about 20 minutes at 350°F (180°C). Do not overcook. Tear open paper and serve hot.

Leftovers are delicious cold and make a good relish for cold beef or chicken.

Recipe courtesy of Carlo Middione, Vivande Porta Via Cafe, San Francisco.

Vegetarian Stock

Instead of beef or chicken, try vegetables for soup stock.

Ingredients

2	medium potatoes, diced, use cleaned peels	3 or 4	sprigs parsley
1	large onion, diced, use cleaned skin	10	peppercorns
2	carrots, sliced ⅛ inch thick		Other vegetable trimmings—bean strings and ends, pea pods, carrot parings, broccoli leaves, mushroom stems
3	ribs celery, thinly sliced		
1	rib broccoli, sliced		
1	whole head garlic, split into unpeeled cloves (skin on)	0	slices fresh ginger
		2	tablespoons olive oil
1	bay leaf		

Method

Combine all the ingredients in a stockpot and cover with water. Bring the mixture to a boil and simmer for about 1½ hours. Strain. If a stronger stock is desired, reduce by boiling vigorously after straining out the vegetables.

Hearty Minestrone
(Serves 8-10)

Ingredients

1/3	cup dried chick peas, rinsed and picked over	1	pound (500 g) Swiss chard or beet greens
1	cup cold water	1/4	pound (125 g) green beans
2	carrots, diced	1	zucchini, cut in 1/4-inch slices
2	stalks celery, diced	1	cup tiny pasta
1	large potato, diced	1	tablespoon minced fresh oregano
1	large red onion, diced	1	tablespoon minced fresh marjoram
1/4	cup olive oil		Salt to taste
4	cups water		Pepper to taste
2	cups chicken stock		Freshly grated Parmesan cheese
1	1-pound (500 g) can Italian plum tomatoes		
3	cloves garlic, minced		

Method

In a large saucepan, cover the chick peas with the water and soak overnight.

Add enough water to cover the chick peas by 1 inch, bring to the boil, and simmer, covered for 1–2 hours, or until tender. Drain, reserving one cup of the liquid.

In a large stainless steel or enamelled kettle, cook the carrots, celery, potato and onion in the olive oil over moderate heat, stirring, for 7 minutes. Add the 4 cups of water, stock, tomatoes and garlic. Bring to the boil and simmer, partially covered, for 25 minutes.

Meanwhile, cut the stems from the Swiss chard or beet greens, reserving the leaves. Cut the stems crosswise into 1-inch pieces. Add the stems and the zucchini to the mixture and simmer, uncovered, for 5 minutes. Stir in the chard leaves or beet greens—torn into pieces, the chick peas, reserved liquid, pasta, oregano, marjoram, salt and pepper to taste. Simmer the soup 10 minutes, stirring. Remove the kettle from the heat and let the soup stand, covered, for 10 minutes.

Ladle the minestrone into heated bowls and serve with freshly grated Parmesan.

Hot and Spicy Black Bean Soup

(Serves 5–6)

Ingredients

½	pound (250 g) black beans	2-3	dried red chili peppers
5	cups water or chicken stock		Salt
1	cup leftover ham, chopped or a ham bone		Chili powder
			Ground cumin
1	large onion, chopped	6	tablespoons sour cream

Method

Wash the beans and pick out any stones. Soak overnight in water to cover. The water will turn grey. Drain the water and discard. Cook the beans in water or stock with ham scraps or bones. Add the onion and chili peppers and cook until the beans are soft. Strain the liquid and reserve. Put the beans through a food mill or meat grinder and make a smooth paste. Add the liquid back to the bean paste until you achieve desired thickness. Add salt, chili powder and ground cumin.

Serve in soup bowls. Add 1 tablespoon of sour cream to each serving.

Chicken Corn Soup

(Serves 4)

Ingredients

3	egg whites	3	tablespoons cornstarch
2	tablespoons evaporated milk	1	teaspoon salt
4	cups chicken broth	1	tablespoon butter
1	14-ounce (398 mL) can creamed corn		

Method

Beat egg whites and milk thoroughly and set aside. In a saucepan, combine the chicken broth with creamed corn. Cook to boiling point. Dilute cornstarch with a bit of chicken broth and add slowly to the boiling mixture. Remove pan from stove. Whisk egg-white mixture into soup, stirring constantly. Taste and add salt, if necessary. Add butter and serve.

Quick Chicken Stock

An easy-to-make stock that stores well.

Ingredients

2½	pounds (1 kg) chicken wings	1	stalk celery
1	onion	8	cups water
1	carrot		

Method

Simmer all of the ingredients in the water in a covered saucepan for 2 hours. Remove chicken and vegetables, strain and chill.

Chilled Buttermilk and Red Pepper Soup

"Why cook with unsalted butter and then add salt to the finished dish?" asks a viewer. Unsalted butter has a stronger taste of fresh butter and therefore enriches the flavor of foods cooked in it. Salted butter disguises the buttery taste. If saltiness is desired, we'd rather add it as seasoning. (Serves 6)

Ingredients

4	cups chopped red pepper	1½	cups chicken stock
2	cups chopped, well-washed leeks	4	cups buttermilk
½	cup unsalted butter		Salt and white pepper

Method

Sauté the red pepper and leeks in butter, in a large, heavy saucepan with a tight-fitting lid, over low heat for 15 minutes or until the vegetables are softened. Add the chicken stock and bring the mixture to the boiling point. Simmer, partially covered, for 30 minutes.

In a blender or food processor fitted with the steel blade, purée the mixture in batches until it is smooth. Pour it into a large bowl and let cool. Stir in the buttermilk and chill the soup, covered, for 4 hours. Taste and season soup with salt and pepper.

Carrot and Thyme Soup

The natural flavor of carrots is heightened with thyme in chicken stock in this puréed soup. Thanks to the food processor, creamed soups needn't be thickened with flour and cream; a purée of cooked vegetables does the trick. The taste is better and, coincidentally, so is the nutritive value. (Serves 6)

Ingredients

1	pound (500 g) fresh carrots	1	tablespoon sugar
1	potato	1	teaspoon salt (optional)
½	onion	½	cup toasted sliced almonds*
4	cups chicken or beef stock		Few gratings fresh pepper
1	tablespoon fresh thyme (1½ teaspoons if using dried)		

Method

Peel and cube the vegetables. Place in a saucepan with stock and fresh thyme. If using dried thyme, make sure it's fresh—smell for flavor and add after the soup has simmered for 15 minutes. Bring to the boil and simmer until soft, about 20 minutes. Remove stalks of thyme. Remove vegetables with a slotted spoon to food processor fitted with metal blade. Add 1 cup broth. Blend until smooth, gradually adding more stock through the feed tube.

Pour back into saucepan. Add sugar and salt to taste. Reheat. Add 1½ tablespoons almonds to each bowl and sprinkle with pepper.

*To toast sliced almonds, lay the almonds flat on a cookie sheet and heat at 350°F (180°C) in a toaster or regular oven until brown—approximately 5–7 minutes.

MEAT

BEEF

VEAL

PORK

LAMB

LEFTOVERS

Winter Stew

There is nothing quite like the rich aroma and flavor of a good beef stew after a hard day on the ski slopes, battling winter traffic, or coping with children's snowsuits. This dish is easy to make, and delicious garnished with parsley and served with salad and fresh Italian bread. (Serves 4-6)

Ingredients

1¼	pounds (625 g) round steak, cut in ½-inch cubes	½	bay leaf
3	tablespoons vegetable oil (corn, safflower, sunflower or other pure vegetable oil)	1	teaspoon oregano
		3	large potatoes, sliced
		3	medium yams, cut in chunks
1	small onion, chopped	1	cup frozen corn, or, in summer, 1 ear fresh corn, sliced in ½-inch rounds
1	tablespoon chopped red pepper		
1	clove garlic, minced	1	medium zucchini, sliced
1½	cups beef stock	6	pitted prunes
2	tablespoons Marsala wine	6	dried apricots, halved
1	10-ounce (284 mL) can tomatoes, well drained		Chopped parsley

Method

Brown meat in half the oil, one-half at a time, in order to allow room for the meat to brown evenly. Remove the meat from the pan; set aside. Sauté the onion, red pepper and garlic in remaining oil. Add the stock and Marsala and bring to a boil. Add the meat and drippings, tomatoes and seasonings. Cover and simmer until the meat is tender, about 1½ hours.

Boil the potatoes and yams and set aside. Fifteen minutes before serving, add the potatoes, yams, fresh corn, and dried fruit, to the meat and cook an additional 10 minutes. If using frozen corn, add it now with zucchini and cook another 5 minutes. Serve sprinkled with chopped parsley.

Note: This stew may be thickened with Beurre Manie (following)

Beurre Manie

Ingredients

1	tablespoon soft butter	1	tablespoon flour

Method

Manipulate the butter and flour with your fingers, as though you were rubbing for fine pastry. Form the mixture into small balls and drop into the hot liquid, stirring constantly until the ingredients are well blended and the sauce thickens.

Stuffed Flank Steak

A slow cooker is best for this dish. (Serves 6)

Ingredients

2	tablespoons butter	½	teaspoon thyme
1	medium onion, chopped		Pinch rosemary
1	clove garlic, minced		Pinch freshly grated black
½	cup sliced mushroom		pepper
¼	cup chopped parsley	½	cup beef broth or bouillon
1½	cups soft fresh bread-crumbs	1½-2	pounds (700 g–1 kg) flank steak

Method

Melt butter in skillet and soften onion and garlic. Add mushrooms and stir. Remove from heat and stir in parsley, breadcrumbs, and seasonings. Mix well. Mixture should have a moist consistency.

Place stuffing in the middle of the steak, roll and tie with string. If the steak is too wide for a slow cooker, cut in two pieces. Place steak in slow cooker and add broth. Cook 8–10 hours on low setting. Remove the meat and slice thinly.

To make gravy, strain the juices from the slow cooker into a small saucepan and bring to a boil. Meanwhile, dilute 2 tablespoons of flour in a small amount of water. Stir into the juices and simmer until thickened. Serve with flank steak.

Note: If you are not using a slow cooker for this dish, sauté the dressed steak in 3 tablespoons of butter until nicely browned. Place on a rack in a small roasting pan and add broth or bouillon. Roast in a preheated 325°F (160°C) oven for 3–4 hours or until fork tender.

Braised Beef Ribs in Rich Tomato Sauce

Use a slow cooker for this recipe. (Serves 6)

Ingredients

2½-3	pounds (1.5 kg) beef short ribs, cut up	2	cloves garlic, minced
	Flour	1	14-ounce (398 mL) can tomatoes
	Salt and pepper	1	teaspoon basil leaves
3-4	tablespoons vegetable oil (corn, safflower, sunflower or other pure vegetable oil)	1	teaspoon oregano leaves
		1	bay leaf
2	medium onions, sliced	½	teaspoon salt
		¼	teaspoon red pepper flakes

Method

Season flour with salt and pepper. Dredge ribs in mixture shaking off excess.

Heat oil in a large skillet. Brown ribs in hot oil. (Two batches may be necessary.) Place browned ribs in slow cooker and add the remaining ingredients. Cover and cook 8–10 hours on low setting, or 4–6 hours on high setting. Remove bay leaf before serving.

To serve, remove ribs to platter and keep warm. Skim off fat from sauce. Sauce may be thickened with 1 tablespoon flour mixed with ¼ cup water. Pour over ribs. Serve with cooked noodles or rice.

Beef in Tortillas with Chile Salsa

This beef mixture is so versatile that you will want to serve it many times—perhaps over rice or with different fresh vegetables. Vegetables and grains, sources of complex carbohydrates, contain important fiber and nutrients including thiamin and niacin. Together, the beef, vegetables, and grains represent three of the four food groups—a tasty beginning to a balanced diet. (Serves 4-6)

Ingredients

1	pound (500 g) beef top round steak	4	tortillas
1	teaspoon vegetable oil	¼	cup chopped parsley
1	onion, chopped	1	large tomato peeled and chopped
1	clove garlic, finely chopped	1	large zucchini, sliced
¼-½	teaspoon Tabasco or other hot red pepper sauce		Sour cream
	Salt, if needed		Chile salsa (see following)

Method

Trim outside layer of fat from steak. Slice steak into thin strips; cut into squares. Heat oil in large sauté pan until hot. Add beef; cook quickly, stirring constantly, until beef is browned on all sides, about 4 minutes. Stir in onion, garlic, and red pepper sauce. Heat to boiling; reduce heat and cover. Simmer 10 minutes or until beef is tender. Taste and add salt, if necessary. Wrap tortillas in foil; heat at 350°F (180°C) until warm, about 6 minutes. Stir parsley into beef mixture. Add tomato and zucchini; cover. Cook just until hot, about 4 minutes. With slotted spoon, place about 1 cup beef mixture in each tortilla. Serve each tortilla with sour cream and chile salsa.

Chile Salsa

(Makes 4 cups or 12 servings)

Ingredients

3	small hot fresh green chilies (serranos or jalapenos)	3	large tomatoes, peeled, cored, seeded and chopped
1	tablespoon chopped fresh cilantro (coriander)	¼	cup vegetable oil
12	green onions including tops, chopped	¼	cup red wine vinegar

Method

Remove stems from chilies and chop finely. Combine chilies, cilantro, onions, tomatoes, oil and vinegar. Can be made only one day in advance. Cover and chill.

Quick Beef Ragout

A dark, delicious stew for two to make when you're in a hurry. Serve with boiled, buttered potatoes or noodles. (Serves 2)

Ingredients

¾	pound (375 g) lean beef, cut into 1-inch pieces	¼	teaspoon basil
1	tablespoon vegetable oil	¼	teaspoon sage
¾	cup dry white wine	3	tablespoons tomato sauce
½	teaspoon salt	1	clove garlic, crushed
¼	teaspoon pepper	1	chopped pimento
¼	teaspoon thyme	2	tablespoons red wine

Method

Sauté the beef in the oil to brown quickly. Add the white wine, salt, pepper, thyme, basil and sage. Simmer, uncovered, for 20 minutes. Watch that the liquid simmers and doesn't evaporate completely. The meat will be glazed and the sauce condensed to a thin layer on the bottom of the pan. Now, add the tomato sauce, garlic, pimento and red wine. Cover. Cook 5–6 minutes more.

Kummel Casserole

Kummel is the German word for caraway—a spice that has been used since antiquity to flavor cakes, breads, cheeses and soups. When the seeds are distilled, the aromatic oil for kummel liqueur is produced. Here, we just use the seeds to add a bit of tang to this easy-to-prepare meal. (Serves 2-3)

Ingredients

2	tablespoons vegetable oil (corn, safflower, sunflower or other pure vegetable oil)	1	cup sour cream
		1/2	teaspoon salt
		1/4	teaspoon pepper
2	large onions, sliced	1/2	teaspoon caraway seeds
1/2	pound (250 g) chopped beef	3-4	slices whole-wheat or rye bread
2	eggs		

Method

Preheat oven to 375°F (190°C). Heat vegetable oil in a pan and sauté the onions until golden. Drain oil, scoop onions out. Wipe pan with paper towel. Heat pan and brown the beef. Drain the fat. Combine meat and onions.

Beat the eggs with the sour cream, salt, pepper and caraway seeds.

Place the bread slices in the bottom of a shallow casserole. Cover with the meat and onions and pour the sauce over. Bake in preheated oven for 20 minutes.

Beef and Cantonese Noodles

(Serves 2)

Ingredients

3/4	pound (750 g) freshly ground beef	2 1/2	teaspoons soy sauce
1	cup sliced onion	1/2	teaspoon salt
1	cup diced celery	1/8	teaspoon pepper
4	tomatoes, quartered		Boiled noodles
1/2	green pepper, chopped		Chopped almonds

Method

Sauté beef in a hot pan with onion, celery, tomatoes and green pepper until onion is soft. Add the soy sauce, salt and pepper. Bring to a boil and simmer for 30 minutes. Serve over boiled noodles. Sprinkle with almonds.

Sweet and Sour Cabbage Rolls—Jewish Style
(Serves 6-8)

Ingredients

Rolls

1	cup rice, cooked for 10 minutes and drained	1/8	teaspoon pepper
1½	pounds (750 g) ground beef chuck	1	small onion, minced
2	teaspoons salt	1	large head cabbage
			Boiling salted water

Sauce

	Beef stock or water	2	tablespoons brown sugar
1	small onion	2	tablespoons tomato paste
6	whole cloves	½	cup raisins
1	bay leaf	8 or 9	gingersnaps, crushed
3	tablespoons lemon juice		

Method

Combine the rice, beef, salt, pepper and onion and blend lightly. Carefully cut core from cabbage. Drop the whole cabbage into boiling salted water. Cook 7–8 minutes until just wilted. Separate leaves carefully. Do not break them. Using a very sharp knife, hold the leaf flat to the cutting board and slice off the thick part of the rib so the leaf will roll more easily. Place a generous tablespoonful of meat mixture on each leaf at rib end. Start to roll, turning in the sides of the leaf, rolling loosely to make a neat cylinder. Secure with wood picks or tie, if desired. Place the rolls fold-side down in a deep kettle and cover with beef stock. Stud the remaining whole small onion with cloves and add to the kettle along with bay leaf, lemon juice, sugar and tomato paste. Cover and simmer 1 hour. Add raisins and crushed gingersnaps and simmer 15 minutes further, stirring occasionally.

Arrange cooked cabbage rolls in a single layer in a 3–4 inch deep baking pan. Add salt and more lemon juice or sugar to taste. Remove bay leaf and onion from sauce, pour over rolls and bake at 375°F (190°C) for 30–40 minutes or until the sauce is thick and rolls are browned.

Ginger and Orange Beef

Light and quick to prepare, this beef stir-fry is high in flavor and low in calories, and if you require a low sodium diet, substitute orange juice for half the soy sauce. (Serves 4)

Ingredients

1	pound (500 g) beef top round steak	1	teaspoon cinnamon
¼	cup soy sauce	2	teaspoons vegetable oil
1½	teaspoons cornstarch	1	carrot, sliced
1½	tablespoons grated orange peel	1	green pepper, sliced
1	tablespoon freshly grated ginger, or 1½ teaspoons ground ginger	1	red pepper, sliced
		¼	pound snow peas, trimmed
		¼	cup sliced water chestnuts
		1	head iceberg lettuce, shredded

Method

Trim outside layer of fat from steak. Slice steak into thin strips. Mix soy sauce, cornstarch, orange peel, ginger and cinnamon. Pour over steak. Heat 1 teaspoon oil in large skillet until hot. Add beef; stir-fry over high heat until browned, about 3 minutes. Remove beef to plate.

Add remaining teaspoon of oil and all vegetables except lettuce. Stir-fry vegetables until crisp-tender, 3–4 minutes. Return beef to skillet. Cook, stirring constantly, until beef is hot. Place lettuce on serving plate; top with beef mixture.

Steak with Oyster Sauce
(Serves 2–3)

Ingredients

1   teaspoon sugar
¼   teaspoon ground white pepper
2   tablespoons light soy sauce
2   tablespoons rice wine or sherry
1   tablespoon vegetable oil
2   cups sliced sirloin steak, ¼ inch thick
⅛   teaspoon salt
¼   cup oyster sauce

½   cup chicken broth
1   tablespoon cornstarch
2   tablespoons vegetable oil
    Salt
2   pieces ginger, shredded
1   clove garlic, minced
3   scallions split in quarters lengthwise, then cut into 1-inch lengths

Method

Combine sugar, white pepper, soy sauce, rice wine or sherry, and vegetable oil. Marinate meat in this mixture for ½ hour.

Combine the salt, oyster sauce, chicken broth and cornstarch.

Drain meat marinade into oyster sauce mixture, set aside. Heat wok, add oil, salt, ginger and garlic. Add meat, fry 1 minute, longer if you prefer meat well done. Remove meat from wok, add scallions and liquid mixture. When gravy thickens, return meat to wok, turn off heat and remove to serving platter.

Savory Liver and Rice

I'll bet you don't believe you can make liver a treat, especially with some family members—surprise, surprise! (Serves 4–5)

Ingredients

¼   cup all-purpose flour
1   teaspoon salt
¼   teaspoon pepper
1   pound (500 g) beef liver
6   slices bacon
2   tablespoons vegetable oil
½   cup chopped onion
½   cup diced celery

1   14-ounce (398 mL) can tomatoes
    Salt
½   teaspoon chili powder
1   cup hot, cooked rice
1   tablespoon parsley, finely chopped

Method

Combine flour, salt and pepper in a small bowl. Cut liver into strips and toss in seasoned flour. Fry bacon for 1 minute. Discard fat and add oil. Add liver, onion and celery. Fry for another 2–3 minutes, or until liver is browned. Add tomatoes and chili powder. Simmer for 10 minutes or until liver is tender, stirring occasionally. Taste sauce and adjust for seasoning, if necessary. Toss rice and parsley and place on hot plate. Pour liver mixture over.

Ground Veal Patties in Sesame Seed Crust

Chef Niels Kjeldson suggested this to me as a delicious way to serve ground lamb. When ground lamb wasn't handy, I improvised with veal. It was terrific. (Serves 4)

Ingredients

1	pound (500 g) ground veal, formed into 16 thin patties	3	tablespoons vegetable oil
	Salt	1	clove garlic
	Pepper	1	teaspoon vegetable oil
2	eggs, lightly beaten	2	teaspoons honey
½	cup sesame seeds	2	teaspoons chopped mint
		½	cup 18% cream

Method

Season the veal patties with salt and pepper. Dip them in egg and then in sesame seeds and set on a plate. Heat a large sauté pan and add oil. Sauté the veal quickly in the hot oil. Remove to a warm platter and keep warm.

In a separate smaller pan, sauté the garlic in the oil over a low heat— do not brown. Add the remaining ingredients and simmer 2 minutes. Pour over veal and serve immediately.

Cha Shao Roast Pork

Here is a crusty, sweet and pungent pork tenderloin cooked Chinese style. Purchase any special ingredients from a Chinese specialty store. (Serves 6)

Ingredients

2	pounds (1 kg) pork tenderloin	1½	tablespoons pale dry sherry
		1	tablespoon hoisin sauce
	Marinade	½	teaspoon honey
1½	tablespoons soy sauce	1	tablespoon oil
1½	teaspoons red bean paste		

Method

Slice the tenderloin lengthwise in half but do not cut right through. It should open flat. Place in a shallow dish. Combine marinade ingredients and pour over the pork. Marinate for at least 2 hours. When ready to serve, preheat the oven to 450°F (230°C). Place pork on a rack in a roasting pan. Roast on the upper rack of the oven for 12 minutes. Turn halfway through roasting time. Remove from oven and cut into ¼-inch slices. The outside will be crusted, the inside moist and juicy. Serve with steamed white rice.

Sweet and Spicy Pork Roast

This one marinates overnight. It's worth the wait!
(Makes 10–12 servings)

Ingredients

1	teaspoon dry mustard	1	1-inch piece ginger root, peeled and halved
1	teaspoon dried thyme		
5	pound (2.3 kg) pork loin roast	½	cup dry sherry
		½	cup light soy sauce
3	cloves garlic, peeled	½	cup red currant jelly

Method

Combine mustard and thyme together between two sheets of waxed paper. Roll with a rolling pin. Coat the pork in the powder and place the meat in a large plastic bag set in a dish.

Finely chop the garlic and ginger, add the sherry and soy sauce. Pour the marinade over the pork and tightly seal the bag. Refrigerate overnight, turning several times.

Remove the pork from the plastic bag to a roasting pan and discard the marinade. Roast the pork at 325°F (165°C) for 20 minutes per pound or until a meat thermometer inserted in the thickest part registers 155°F-160°F (68°-71°C). Remove from the oven and set the pork on a platter.

Melt the jelly in a small saucepan and spoon over the pork.

Leg of Spring Lamb with Spinach, Apricot and Walnut Stuffing

Now that boned legs of lamb are readily available, it is simple to create new dishes with interesting and subtle tastes. Lamb can be stuffed with a variety of flavorful dressings—sometimes sweet, other times delicately spiced—to enhance its robust taste. (Serves 6-8)

Ingredients

4	pounds (2 kg) leg spring lamb, boned with fat removed	½	cup chopped dried apricots
	Salt	½	cup chopped walnuts
	Freshly ground pepper	1	egg, beaten
2	tablespoons butter	2	tablespoons 10% cream
1	garlic clove, minced	1	tablespoon Madeira, port wine or beef stock
1	onion, finely chopped	1	teaspoon grated orange rind
1	package fresh spinach, cooked, drained and chopped	¼	teaspoon freshly grated nutmeg
1	cup fresh breadcrumbs	1	teaspoon Dijon mustard

Method

Sprinkle boned lamb with salt and freshly ground pepper. Melt butter in a large frying pan, add garlic and onion and cook until softened.

In a large bowl combine onion and garlic with the remaining ingredients and mix well. Spread the stuffing over leg; roll and tie securely. Insert meat thermometer into meat (not stuffing). Roast on a rack at 350°F (180°C) for 1-2 hours or until the internal temperature registers 160°F (70°C). Remove the roast to a warm platter.

Pour off the fat from roasting pan and deglaze with a little more Madeira, port wine, or beef stock to make a sauce from the pan juices.

Lamb with White Beans

Lamb cut from the shoulder or leg and combined with beans makes a tasty, economical dish in the style of the robust fare of southwestern France. (Serves 4-6)

Ingredients

1½	pounds (750 g) lamb, cubed, visible fat removed	1	tablespoon tomato paste
	Salt	1	piece lemon peel
	Freshly ground pepper	½	pound (250 g) dry white beans (1 cup)
	Sugar	1	carrot, sliced
2	tablespoons olive oil	1	onion, studded with 2 cloves
¼	pound (125 g) lean salt pork, blanched and diced, or bacon, diced	1	bouquet garni (celery stalk, parsley, bay leaf and thyme wrapped in cheesecloth)
1	cup chopped onions (2 medium)	1	pound (500 g) garlic sausage, cut in 1-inch pieces
2	cloves garlic, minced	½	cup soft breadcrumbs
½	cup dry red wine	1	tablespoon olive oil
1	pound (500 g) ripe tomatoes, peeled, seeded and chopped or 1 cup canned tomatoes, drained	2	tablespoons chopped parlsey

Method

Sprinkle lamb cubes with salt, pepper and a pinch of sugar. Brown well, in a single layer, in hot olive oil in a large heavy frying pan. Set aside. Discard browning oil.

Brown salt pork or bacon in frying pan; remove. Add the onions and garlic to pan; cook until softened. Stir in red wine and bring to a boil. Reduce heat and add tomatoes, tomato paste and lemon peel.

Return lamb and pork pieces to the pan. Cover and simmer until lamb is tender, about 1 hour. Set aside.

Meanwhile, rinse beans, then cover with cold water (three times as much water as beans). Bring to a boil. Boil 2 minutes and set aside for 1 hour. Drain and cover again with water as before. Tuck the carrot, onion with cloves and bouquet garni into the beans. Return to boil and simmer, covered. After 1 hour, prick the garlic sausage in several places and add to the bean pot. Simmer ½ hour more.

In a large casserole dish, place a layer of beans, cover with a few pieces of sausage and half of the lamb pieces. Repeat bean, sausage and lamb layer and finish with a bean layer. Add all the juices from the meat and some of the bean stock to moisten mixture. Toss the breadcrumbs with olive oil and sprinkle over the casserole. Set uncovered in a 350°F (170°C) oven for about 1 hour, until casserole is heated through and a crisp brown topping has formed. Sprinkle with parsley.

Tarragon Lamb Chops

Although native to southern Europe, tarragon grows well and thrives throughout the temperate climates. Of the two types of tarragon, French and Russian, the French variety is considered to have a finer flavor but is more difficult to cultivate. Fresh or dried tarragon has many uses: in mayonnaise-type sauces, in stuffings for poultry and meat and in sauces for fish, veal, chicken and lamb. (Serves 4)

Ingredients

4	loin lamb chops	1	tablespoon fresh tarragon, chopped
½	teaspoon salt		
¼	teaspoon black pepper	8	tarragon sprays
4	tablespoons olive oil	4	tomatoes, halved

Method

Sprinkle the chops with salt and pepper, rubbing the seasoning in with your fingertip. Place the chops in a shallow dish.

In a small mixing bowl, combine the oil and chopped tarragon. Pour the oil mixture over the chops and set aside for 30 minutes.

Heat the broiler to high. Place the chops on the rack of the broiler pan and place 2 tarragon sprays on each chop. Place the tomatoes on the edge of the rack. Broil the chops for 2 minutes on each side. Reduce the heat to moderately low and broil the chops for an additional 10 minutes on each side or until the chops are tender when pierced with the point of a sharp knife and the tomatoes are cooked. During broiling, brush the chops frequently with the oil marinade.

Remove the chops and the tomatoes from the broiler and place them on a warmed serving plate. Serve immediately.

Roast of Spring Lamb
(Serves 4)

Ingredients

1	2-pound (1 kg) crown roast spring lamb	½	pound (250 g) onions
1	clove garlic, halved	¾	pound (375 g) green peppers
	Olive oil	1½	pounds (750 g) fresh ripe tomatoes, or 2 cups drained, canned tomatoes
1	tablespoon lemon juice		
	Salt	2	cloves garlic, minced
	Freshly ground pepper	1	teaspoon dried basil
½	teaspoon thyme	1	tablespoon chopped fresh parsley
1	large eggplant		
	Salt		Salt to taste
1	pound (500 g) zucchini		

Method

Rub all the surfaces of lamb with a cut garlic clove, a little olive oil, the lemon juice and a sprinkling of salt, pepper and thyme. Stand at room temperature for about 1 hour or refrigerate until required.

Meanwhile, prepare vegetable mixture. Peel eggplant, cut into 1-inch sections; sprinkle lightly with salt and set aside. Trim and scrub zucchini; cut and salt in the same way. Peel and slice onions. Slice and seed peppers. Peel, seed and slice tomatoes. Heat a small amount of olive oil in a large fry pan; wipe eggplant slices to remove salt and moisture and brown all sides. Remove. Add more oil as necessary, brown zucchini in the same way. Remove and set aside. Toss onions and peppers into fry pan and cook for 5 minutes until lightly brown, then stir in tomatoes. Season lightly, add a pinch of thyme and cook several minutes until the tomatoes are tender and some of the juices are reduced.

Return eggplant and zucchini to the pan with the remaining garlic and herbs. Stir gently to combine; simmer for about 20 minutes, uncovered, basting occasionally with the fragrant cooking juices until vegetables are just tender but still retain their shape and bright color. Set aside and reheat before serving.

Line the cavity of the roast with aluminum foil, then place in a preheated 400°F (200°C) oven. Immediately reduce heat to 350°F (180°C). Roast for 45 minutes–1 hour, or until internal temperature reaches 160°F (70°C). Remove roast to a warm platter. Sprinkle with salt. Discard foil from the cavity and fill with vegetable mixture, spooning the rest into a casserole. Carve down between the ribs and serve with spoonfuls of remaining vegetables. Crisp roasted or sautéed potatoes would make a delicious accompaniment.

Low calorie version: Omit the olive oil and steam the eggplant and zucchini using a steamer or microwave oven. Steam for five minutes or until the vegetables are crisp but tender. Sauté onions and pepper in a small amount of oil or use a non-stick frying pan.

Lamb and Zucchini Kebabs
(Serves 6)

Ingredients

1	cup vegetable oil	2	teaspoons dried tarragon
⅓	cup fresh lemon juice	1	teaspoon salt
3	scallions, including green tops, thinly sliced	1½	pounds (750 g) boneless lamb shoulder, trimmed and cut into 1½-inch cubes
2	teaspoons tarragon or Dijon mustard	3	zucchini, scrubbed and cut into 1-inch pieces
2	tablespoons fresh tarragon, minced, *or*		

Method

In a shallow ceramic or glass dish combine the oil, lemon juice, scallions, mustard, tarragon and salt. Add the lamb and zucchini, tossing them to coat with marinade. Let lamb and zucchini marinate, covered and chilled, at least 6 hours or overnight. Toss occasionally.

Drain the lamb and zucchini, and reserve the marinade. Thread alternate pieces of lamb and zucchini on skewers. Baste the kebabs with reserved marinade and barbecue, turning them, for 25 minutes or until the lamb is cooked medium-rare.

To broil in the oven
Heat broiler for 10 minutes. Drain the kebabs from the marinade and broil, 3 inches from heat, for 40 minutes, turning often.

Lamb Chops with Feta Cheese

Quick and delicious, here is a main dish that is ready in minutes. It can be prepared without the Feta, but for a very new and special taste, add the cheese. (Serves 2)

Ingredients

4	loin or shoulder lamb chops		Freshly ground pepper
1	large clove garlic, chopped	¼	cup drained, crumbled Feta cheese
2–3	teaspoons dried oregano		
2	tablespoons lemon juice		

Method

Heat a sauté pan that has a lid over high heat and add lamb chops. Brown them well on both sides. Sprinkle the garlic over the chops along with the oregano, lemon juice and pepper. Lower heat. Sprinkle with crumbled Feta cheese, cover and cook for 10 minutes, until the cheese melts.

Quick Lamb Pilaf

(Serves 4)

Ingredients

3	cups cooked rice, made with strong bouillon	1	clove garlic, minced
3	tablespoons raisins	2	tomatoes, diced
¼	teaspoon saffron	1	4-ounce (113 mL) can pimentos, drained and diced
1	large onion, sliced	1	cup cooked lamb
1	banana, sliced		
2	tablespoons vegetable oil (corn, sunflower, safflower or other pure vegetable oil)		

Method

Mix together cooked rice, raisins and saffron.

Sauté the sliced onion and banana in oil. Add garlic, tomatoes, pimentos and lamb. Cook 5 minutes. Add the rice, heat and stir 5 minutes more. Serve with a bowl of cold yogurt or sour cream.

Lemon Beef Salad

A tender, succulent roast from last evening's meal is the start of a light, yet satisfying meal the second time around. Begin with cooked beef, trimmed of excess fat. Thinly slice the beef and marinate in a zesty, flavorful mixture of lemon juice and poppy seeds. Fresh vegetables combine with beef for an appetizing, colorful entrée for under 400 calories. (Serves 4)

Ingredients

¼	cup lemon juice	⅔	cup sour cream or yogurt
2	tablespoons water	1	teaspoon Dijon-style mustard
2	tablespoons sugar	1	head red leaf lettuce
1	teaspoon poppy seeds	1	tomato, cut into wedges
¼	teaspoon salt	4	small artichokes, halved, cooked or canned
2	cups cooked roast beef cut into strips		
4	ounces fresh mushrooms, sliced (about 1 cup)		

Method

In saucepan, mix lemon juice, water, sugar, poppy seeds and salt. Heat to boiling; reduce heat and cover. Simmer 15 minutes and cool. In large bowl, mix lemon mixture, beef and mushrooms; cover. Refrigerate at least 3 hours, no longer than 24 hours.

Drain beef mixture; reserve 3 tablespoons marinade. Stir reserved marinade into sour cream or yogurt; stir in mustard. Arrange beef, mushrooms, tomato and artichokes on bed of lettuce. Serve yogurt marinade dressing on the side.

Corn-Stuffed Peppers
(Serves 2)

Ingredients

3 large green peppers
½ cup cooked rice
1 12-ounce (341 mL) can drained corn kernels, or 1 cup leftover corn scraped from cob
1 tablespoon chili sauce
2 teaspoons chili powder

Any leftover meats, finely chopped
¼ cup breadcrumbs
3 tablespoons beef or chicken stock
¼ teaspoon pepper

Method

Preheat oven to 400°F (200°C). Cut tops off the green peppers, remove seeds and fibers and drop into boiling salted water to blanch for 5 minutes. Drain. Prepare the rice and add all the other ingredients. Taste and adjust seasoning. Stuff peppers.

Place upright in a greased dish and bake for 25 minutes, or microwave at medium power for 7 minutes.

If using cold stuffing and unblanched peppers, bake for 15 minutes longer.

POULTRY

Basic Chicken Sauté with Variations

Perfectly sautéed chicken is simple once you master the technique of browning the broilers in a hot pan using clarified butter or a light pure vegetable oil such as corn, soy, sunflower or cottonseed. Since I prefer the taste of butter, I use clarified butter to brown the chicken pieces and then drain away the fat. The bits of browned chicken in the pan are then used to make a rich, fragrant and full-bodied sauce for the dish. Try the basic sauté and then experiment with flavors of your own, or if you'd rather, use our variations as guides.

(Serves 4)

Ingredients

3–4	tablespoons clarified, unsalted butter (see note below)			Freshly ground black pepper
1	3-pound (1.5 kg) chicken, cut into 8 pieces		1	cup chicken stock
	Salt		⅓	cup 35% cream (optional)

Method

Heat the clarified butter in a large, heavy frypan. Pat the chicken dry with a paper towel. Arrange as many chicken pieces as will fit, without touching, skin side down in the hot frypan (if chicken pieces are crowded in pan, they will not brown). Cook over medium to medium-high heat, adjusting the temperature as necessary to produce a popping sound. Chicken should be golden brown in 8–10 minutes. Turn pieces with tongs (do not use fork). Brown second side, about 6–8 minutes. Remove the pieces from pan to drain on paper towel. Continue browning until all chicken is done. Drain off all but 3 tablespoons of the drippings. Return all chicken pieces to the frypan, arranging leg pieces on the bottom and breast pieces on top (dark meat takes longer to cook). Cover frypan; reduce heat to medium-low. Cook until the meat is firm—not springy, when pressed with finger, 10–15 minutes for breast meat, 20–25 minutes for leg meat. Remove the chicken pieces as they are done. When all the chicken is cooked, return them to the frypan for a few minutes to warm through. Sprinkle with salt and pepper. Remove chicken to a heated platter and cover with aluminum foil to keep warm.

Pour off as much fat as possible from frypan. Add stock and cook over high heat. With a wooden spoon scrape up brown bits that cling to the bottom and sides of skillet. Boil until the stock is reduced to ⅓ cup. Add cream and boil, stirring constantly, until the sauce is thick and rich.

Clarified Butter
(Makes ⅔ cup)

Melt 1 cup unsalted butter in a small saucepan over low-medium heat and allow to settle. Remove foam from the top. Pour the yellow liquid (oil) into a container and discard the white milky solids at the bottom. The oil will solidify when chilled and may be used for all sautéing and pan frying. Store covered in the refrigerator. It will keep for 1 month. Clarified butter has a higher burning point than regular butter so that you may pan fry at high temperature without smoking and burning.

VARIATION 1
Sautéed Chicken with Mushrooms

(Serves 4)

Ingredients

1	3-pound (1.5 kg) chicken, cut into 8 pieces	2	green onions, chopped, with tops
3–4	tablespoons clarified, unsalted butter	2	shallots, minced
	Salt	½	cup dry white wine
	Freshly ground black pepper	1	cup chicken stock
8	fresh mushrooms, cut in ¼-inch slices	2	tablespoons cognac or brandy

Method

Brown chicken in clarified butter and cook until firm as in Basic Chicken recipe (see p. 32). Remove chicken to heated platter; sprinkle with salt and pepper. Keep warm.

Pour off all but 1 tablespoon of fat from frypan. Increase heat to medium-high. Add mushrooms, onions and shallots; sauté until mushrooms are golden brown, about 5 minutes. Deglaze frypan with wine; boil until reduced by half. Add stock and cognac and boil until sauce has thickened and is rich in flavor, about 4 minutes. Taste and adjust seasonings. Pour sauce over chicken before serving.

VARIATION 2
Sautéed Chicken with Apricots and Brandy

(Serves 4)

Ingredients

1	3-pound (1.5 kg) chicken, cut into 8 pieces		Salt
3–4	tablespoons clarified, unsalted butter		Freshly ground black pepper
2	large shallots, minced	⅓	cup chicken stock
½	cup dried apricots	3	tablespoons 35% cream
¼	cup + 1 tablespoon apricot or other fruit brandy		

Method

Brown chicken in clarified butter, as in Basic Chicken Sauté (see p. 32). Return chicken to frypan, breast pieces on top. Sprinkle with shallots, apricots and the 1 tablespoon of brandy. Cook until chicken is firm. Remove chicken to heated platter; sprinkle with salt and pepper. Keep warm.

Degrease pan drippings. Deglaze frypan with the ¼ cup brandy; boil until reduced by half. Add stock and cream and boil until the sauce is thickened and rich in flavor. Taste and adjust seasonings. Pour sauce over chicken before serving.

VARIATION 3

Sautéed Chicken with Lemon and Zucchini

(Serves 4)

Ingredients

1	tablespoon finely shredded lemon zest	1	teaspoon salt
1	3-pound (1.5 kg) chicken, cut into 8 pieces	⅛	teaspoon freshly ground pepper
3–4	tablespoons clarified, unsalted butter	2	medium zucchini peeled and cut into julienne strips
4	large shallots, minced	½	cup chicken stock
3	tablespoons fresh lemon juice	¼	cup sour cream or yogurt
½	teaspoon dried thyme, crumbled		

Method

Blanch the lemon zest in boiling water for 5 minutes. Drain thoroughly; reserve.

Brown the chicken in clarified butter. Remove chicken from frypan. Pour off all but 1 tablespoon of fat. Add shallots; sauté until lightly browned, about 4 minutes. Return chicken to frypan, breast pieces on top. Sprinkle with the lemon juice, thyme, salt, pepper, and lemon zest. Sauté until chicken is firm. Remove chicken to heated platter; keep warm. Degrease pan drippings. Add zucchini; cook over medium-high heat until heated through, about 4 minutes. Remove zucchini with slotted spoon and scatter over chicken. Deglaze frypan with stock; boil until reduced by half. Remove from heat. Whisk until slightly cooled then pour in sour cream or yogurt. Pour sauce over chicken immediately and serve.

Quick Lemon Chicken
(Serves 3-4)

Ingredients

5-6	Chinese dried mushrooms		5	green onions, thinly sliced
1	3-4-pound (1.5 kg) chicken, boned and cut into bite-sized pieces		¼	cup rice wine or pale, dry sherry
1½	teaspoons salt		1½	teaspoons sugar
	Black pepper, freshly ground		2	tablespoons light-flavored soy sauce
5	tablespoons oil		1	teaspoon cornstarch dissolved in 1 tablespoon water
4	slices ginger root, chopped			
1	red pepper, shredded		1-2	tablespoons lemon juice
	Zest of 2 lemons, grated			

Method

Put the dried mushrooms in a small bowl, cover with warm water and set aside to soak until soft, about 20 minutes. Drain. Cut off and discard the stems. Cut the mushrooms into bite-size pieces. Set aside.

Rub chicken pieces with salt and pepper and 1½ tablespoons oil. Heat 2 tablespoons oil in wok. Add chicken, stir-fry, remove and keep warm. Add remaining oil, heat and add ginger, red pepper and drained mushrooms. Stir-fry 1 minute. Add lemon zest and green onions; stir-fry 30 seconds. Sprinkle in rice wine or sherry, sugar and soy sauce. When mixture comes to boil, stir in cornstarch mixture. Return chicken to wok, sprinkle in lemon juice and serve hot with steamed rice.

Spicy Chicken and Peppers

This spicy chicken dish originated in Turkey, where hot and sweet spices are used to enhance the natural flavors of the food during long cooking. We use it as a main dish with steamed rice or as an appetizer, wrapped in filo pastry and served hot as a first course.

Be sure your spices are fresh, the saffron of good quality and the chicken stock full-bodied*. In our family's opinion, it's better to overspice this dish.

Ingredients

Filling

1	3½–4-pound (1.7–1.8 kg) chicken, quartered or cut in 8 pieces		Pinch saffron
1	carrot, peeled and chopped	4	cups red pepper slices
½	large onion	2	tablespoons butter
1½	cups rich chicken stock	½	cup Italian parsley leaves (cilantro) or, if unavailable, ½ teaspoon coriander seeds
	Pinch saffron		
1	2-inch stick cinnamon	½	cup toasted slivered almonds or pine nuts
2	cloves garlic, crushed		
1	1-inch piece ginger, chopped	½	cup raisins
2	teaspoons cardamom seeds, crushed		Salt to taste (easy on the salt)
			Pepper to taste
1	bay leaf		Pinches of cinnamon and ginger to taste or ½ teaspoon grated fresh ginger
1	tablespoon lemon juice		
1	tablespoon flour		
½	cup 18% cream	1	tablespoon curry powder (optional)
1	clove garlic, minced		

Method

Simmer chicken with the carrot, onion, spices, and lemon juice in the stock for 30–40 minutes or until just tender. Remove and cool chicken pieces. Let the spices simmer 15-20 minutes longer, then strain, reserving broth. Cook the broth down rapidly. Stir the flour into the cream and add the mixture to the broth along with the 1 clove of minced garlic and pinch of saffron. Cook down to about 1 cup by boiling rapidly.

Meanwhile, remove the chicken meat from skin and bones and cut into bite-sized pieces. Cook red pepper slices in the butter; mix in the pieces of chicken, the parsley, almonds and raisins. Salt and pepper to taste and add a pinch of cinnamon or ginger and curry powder. Mix together with the sauce, taste, adjust seasoning and serve.

---

*Homemade chicken stock made from scraps and bones is always best; canned chicken stock is an acceptable substitute, but *taste* as you're cooking for saltiness and intensity of flavor. Don't over salt.

To Serve in Filo

Ingredients

14 sheets 9" x 13" filo dough, store-bought or homemade (see pp. 74-78)

½ cup clarified butter

Method

Cool chicken in refrigerator or to room temperature.

Line a 9" X 13" buttered baking pan crosswise with 8 layers of filo, brushing clarified butter between each piece. Let the extra dough hang over the side. Put in the cooled filling and bring the extra dough over it. Lay 6 more sheets of filo over top, brushing butter between each sheet. Tuck under the sides. Bake at 400°F (200°C) for 15 minutes, then reduce heat to 375°F (190°C) for 20 minutes longer. Serve hot.

Quick Baked Chicken

There are times when simple recipes are best. Here is a recipe for chicken that is simplicity itself. Served with lemon pilaf and almonds, it is a delicious, foolproof party dish. (Serves 4)

Ingredients

1 3-4-pound (1.5-2 kg) chicken
¼ cup melted butter
½ cup honey
¼ cup prepared mustard

1 teaspoon salt
1 teaspoon prepared curry powder

Method

Mix the marinade ingredients together. Dip the chicken pieces in marinade and coat well. Leave refrigerated for about 1 hour, if possible. Place in a flat casserole dish. Bake, uncovered, at 375°F (190°C) for 1 hour.

Steamed Chicken and Pears in Ginger Sauce

When you need a delicious but simple dinner as a welcome reward after a hard day's work, try this—steamed chicken breasts that cook in 10 minutes, low in calories and satisfying to taste. For calorie watchers, this can be served on a bed of finely chopped lettuce; for others, with steamed rice. (Serves 2-3)

Ingredients

1   pound (500 g) boned chicken breasts (about 4 boneless breasts)

2   fresh hard pears, cut in quarters and cored

Ginger sauce (see below)

½   cup sesame seeds

Method

Remove skin and visible fat from breasts. Place breasts between 2 sheets of waxed paper and pound with a mallet to even out. They should be no thinner than ½ inch. This step is not essential but prevents the thinner, more quickly cooked outer sections from burning.

Place the breasts on a dish and set the dish on a trivet or rack in a large pot. Add boiling water below, but not to cover chicken. Cover and steam 5 minutes, add pears and continue cooking 5 minutes longer, or until pears are tender. Line a platter with lettuce or rice. Arrange chicken and pears over top. Drizzle with ginger sauce and sprinkle with sesame seeds.

Ginger Sauce

Ingredients

2   tablespoons sugar
2   teaspoons cornstarch
⅓   cup water
2   tablespoons soy sauce
1–2   teaspoons finely grated ginger root

1   medium clove garlic, minced
1   teaspoon vinegar

Method

Combine all of the ingredients in a saucepan. Bring to a boil and cook over medium heat, stirring constantly until thick and clear. Cool.

Garlic Spiced Chicken

The versatility of chicken provides the cook with a wonderful opportunity to use different flavor combinations. In this dish, chicken is marinated and simmered in a lemon-soy mixture and browned in oil afterwards. It is full-bodied enough for hearty eaters and tasty enough for kids and fussy eaters. Serve with brown or white rice and a sweet vegetable such as gingered carrots or parsnip patties for a complete dinner. (Serves 4)

Ingredients

⅓	cup vinegar		4	stalks celery and leaves, chopped
⅓	cup lemon juice			
3	tablespoons soy sauce		¼	cup all-purpose flour
½-¾	teaspoon black peppercorns		3	tablespoons vegetable oil
8	cloves garlic, minced		1	3-pound (1.5 kg) chicken, cut up
4	bay leaves, crumbled			

Method

Combine the vinegar, lemon juice, soy sauce, peppercorns, garlic, bay leaves and celery. Marinate the chicken 12–24 hours, turning occasionally.

Bring chicken and marinade mixture to boil in a deep saucepan. Simmer, covered, until chicken is barely tender, about 30 minutes or microwave at medium power for 15 minutes. Remove the chicken from pan and drain marinade in sieve, saving only the liquid. Cool the chicken slightly. Coat each piece of chicken lightly with flour. Brown in hot oil on both sides in a heavy skillet. Pour marinade over chicken. Cook over low heat until sauce is reduced by about one-half and chicken is tender.

Rijsttaffel Curry for Company

The word *curry* is derived from applying a Western accent to the Indian word *kari*, which can mean one of two things: the sweet aromatic leaves of the kari plant; or the cooking method used in southwestern India regional cooking for preparing stir-fried vegetables. But what we have learned to call curry is not Indian *kari* at all. Our curry dishes take their name from *salan* (spicy thin gravy), which includes spices such as cardamom and funugreek—not found in traditional *kari*. Still, the main point is flavor, and the flavor of this dish is superb. (Serves 4-6)

Ingredients

1½ chickens, cut into 12 pieces
   Flour, salt and pepper
6 tablespoons clarified butter
3 large onions, chopped
2 cloves garlic, minced
2 tablespoons curry powder
1 teaspoon chili powder
¼ teaspoon cinnamon
¼ teaspoon ginger
2½ cups chicken stock
1 14-ounce (398 mL) can
   tomatoes

3 tablespoons finely chopped
   chutney
½ cup raisins
   Salt and pepper
½ cup slivered almonds
½ cup milk or cream
1 cup diced cucumber
   Juice of ½ lemon
   Hot cooked rice

Method

Dredge chicken in seasoned flour. Brown in 4 tablespoons butter, then remove. Sauté onions and garlic in butter, adding the other 2 tablespoons of butter, if necessary. Add seasonings and sauté a few minutes.Add the chicken stock, tomatoes, chutney, raisins, salt and pepper to taste. Bring to a boil, add the chicken, cover and lower heat. Simmer 1 hour.

Remove chicken from bones and cut into small pieces.

Meanwhile sauté the almonds in 1 tablespoon butter. Place in blender with the cream or milk and then add to the chicken along with the cucumber. Simmer over low heat another ½ hour, until thick. If the mixture becomes too dry, add more chicken stock. Just before serving, add the lemon juice. Serve with rice and any of the following condiments.

Mango chutney, both mild and hot
Diced hard-cooked egg white
Diced hard-cooked egg yolk
Shredded, crisp, fried bacon
Minced mild onion
Minced sweet pepper

Shredded fresh pineapple
Raisins
Bananas fried in cinnamon and butter
Peeled diced cucumber
Diced candied ginger

Kelly's Asian Chicken

This absolutely mouth watering chicken dish is a simple inspired combination that takes only 20 minutes to put together. It was the unanimous first-place choice in the 1981 Garlic Festival Recipe Contest.* Serve with cooked Chinese noodles—and then stand back and let the compliments fly!

Ingredients

1	3½-pound (1.3 kg) frying chicken, cut into serving pieces, or equivalent in chicken pieces of your choice	1	bulb fresh garlic, peeled and coarsely chopped
3	tablespoons peanut or other pure vegetable oil (corn, safflower, sunflower)	2	small, dried, hot red peppers (optional)
		¾	cup mild white vinegar
		¼	cup soy sauce
		3	tablespoons honey

Method

Heat the oil in a large, heavy skillet and brown the chicken well on all sides, adding garlic and peppers towards the end. Add remaining ingredients and cook over medium-high heat until chicken is done and sauce has been reduced a little. This will not take long, less than 10 minutes.

It you are cooking both white and dark meat, remove white meat first, so it does not dry out. Be sure not to let the sauce burn or boil away. There should be enough sauce left to serve with the chicken; and the chicken should appear slightly glazed.

Serve with Chinese noodles, pasta or rice.

---

*Garlic Festival recipe contest winner: Kelly Greene, Mill Valley, 1981. Courtesy of California Garlic Association.

Paella à la Valenciana

Noted Spanish food authority and cookbook author, Penelope Casas, gave us this recipe for paella. It is as authentic as possible for North American food markets, and will guide you to a perfectly superb dinner presentation. Be sure to use a large, flat, heavy paella pan with about a 15-inch base, or, failing this, use a cast-iron frying pan—one that can be put in the oven for baking. The rice must be imported short-grain rice and the ham uncooked, like proscuitto.

Ingredients

6	cups very strong chicken broth, preferably homemade	2	tomatoes, chopped
½	teaspoon saffron	2	pimentos, diced
1	onion, peeled	1	pound small or medium shrimp, *shelled*
18	clams, smallest available, at room temperature, scrubbed	2	live lobsters, split and divided into tail sections and claws (discard the head and small claws); or 4 lobster tails, split lengthwise; or 8 king crab claws; or 8 jumbo shrimp, *in their shells*
1	4-pound (2 kg) chicken		
	Coarse salt		
½	cup olive oil		
¼	pound chorizo sausage, cut in ¼-inch slices		
		3	cups short-grain rice
1	large pork chop, boned and diced	5	tablespoons parsley, chopped
		2	bay leaves, crumbled
¼	pound piece cured ham, diced	½	cup dry white wine
1	medium onion, chopped	1	tablespoon lemon juice
4	scallions, chopped	¼	pound peas, fresh or frozen
4	cloves garlic, minced	18	mussels, small, scrubbed

Garnish

Lemon wedges   Chopped parsley

Method

Heat the broth with the saffron and the whole onion. Add the cleaned clams, cover and simmer 15 minutes. Remove the onion and clams to a bowl, and measure the broth—you need exactly 5½ cups. Reserve. Cut the chicken into small serving pieces—the whole breast in 4 parts, each thigh into 2 parts, the bony tip of the leg chopped off, the wing discarded, and the rest of the wing separated into 2 parts. Remove fat and skin when chopping for fewer calories. Dry the pieces well and sprinkle with salt. In a metal paella pan, heat the oil very well. Add the chicken pieces and fry over high heat until golden. Remove to a warm platter.

Add the chorizo, pork and ham to the pan and stir-fry about 10 minutes. Add the chopped onion, scallions, garlic, pimentos and tomatoes and sauté until the onion is wilted. Add the shrimp and lobster and sauté about 3 minutes more, or until the shrimp and the lobster barely turn pink (the lobster will cook more in the oven). Remove the shrimp and lobster to the platter with the chicken. Add the rice to the pan and stir to coat it well with the oil. *Note:* There should be no more than 1½-2 inches of rice in the pan. The rice should form a crust on the bottom by the end of the cooking. Sprinkle in the 5 tablespoons chopped parsley and the crumbled bay leaves. (May be made in advance up to this point.)

Stir in the chicken broth, boiling hot, the wine, lemon juice, and peas. Salt to taste. Bring to a boil and cook, uncovered and stirring occasionally, over medium-high heat about 10 minutes. Bury the shrimp and the chicken in the rice.

Add the mussels, pushing them into the rice, with the edge that will open facing up. Decorate the paella with the lobster pieces and clams then bake at 325°F (160°C), uncovered, for 20 minutes. Remove from the oven and let sit on top of the stove, lightly covered with foil for about 10 minutes. To serve, decorate with lemon wedges and chopped parsley.

Chicken with Baby Corn
(Serves 3–4)

Ingredients

4	Chinese dried mushrooms	1	14-ounce (398 mL) can baby corn, drained
2	chicken breasts		
1	egg white	¼	cup baby peas, or snow pea pods
1	teaspoon salt		
2	tablespoons dry sherry	¼	cup chicken stock
1	tablespoon cornstarch	1	tablespoon soy sauce
2	tablespoons vegetable oil (corn, safflower, sunflower or other pure vegetable oil)	1	teaspoon sesame oil

Method

Soak the Chinese mushrooms in warm water to cover for 15 minutes. Drain, squeeze out moisture and shred. Set aside.

Skin and bone the chicken breasts and cut chicken meat into 1-inch pieces. Mix the chicken with egg white, salt, sherry and cornstarch. Set aside.

Heat the oil in a wok until very hot and stir-fry the chicken for 2 minutes. Add the vegetables and stir. Add stock and soy sauce and cook, covered 3–4 minutes. Drizzle sesame oil over top and serve immediately with steamed or boiled rice.

Chicken and Artichoke Casserole

There are as many recipes for this casserole as recipes for brownies; this is mine and I stand firmly behind it as my favorite. Once prepared, the casserole rests all day in the refrigerator ready to be baked for company in the evening. (Serves 6)

Ingredients

1	3-pound (1.5 kg) chicken, cut into 8 pieces	2	tablespoons flour
½	teaspoon paprika	½	teaspoon dried oregano
¼	teaspoon ground white pepper	2	6-ounce (170 mL) jars mari-nated artichokes
1	teaspoon salt	⅓	cup chicken stock
3	tablespoons clarified butter	⅓	cup dry sherry
2	tablespoons vegetable oil	2	medium tomatoes, quartered, or 6 cherry tomatoes
2	tablespoons clarified butter		
1½	cups sliced fresh mushrooms		

Method

Sprinkle the chicken pieces with paprika, pepper and salt. Heat a large, flat sauté or frypan and melt 3 tablespoons butter and oil until hot. Add chicken pieces, being careful not to crowd them. If the pan is small, brown the chicken in batches. To brown well, the oil and butter should spatter.

After the chicken is well browned, remove the chicken to a casserole; drain the fat and add two tablespoons clarified butter to the pan. Sauté the mushrooms until golden; add flour and stir. While stirring sprinkle with oregano and add the drained artichoke liquid, stock, sherry and tomatoes. Cook for five minutes.

Arrange the drained artichokes over the chicken in the casserole and pour finished sauce overtop. The dish can now be covered and refrigerated for reheating later.

When ready to serve, heat oven to 375°F (190°C). Bake, covered for 40 minutes.

Broccoli and Chicken Gratin

The quantities of broccoli and chicken can be varied in this recipe as long as the balance of flavors is not lost—don't overwhelm the more subtle flavor of the chicken with too much broccoli.

Ingredients

1½–2	cups cooked white meat of chicken, cut in strips		⅓	cup 35% cream
				Salt
1	pound (500 g) broccoli, par-boiled			Pepper
				Grated nutmeg
1½	cups medium white sauce (see below)		¼	cup grated Parmesan cheese
1½	cups chicken stock		¼	cup breadcrumbs
1	teaspoon dried tarragon		1	tablespoon butter
4–6	tablespoons dry white vermouth or white wine			

Method

Spread the strips of chicken in a lightly buttered, shallow casserole. Arrange the broccoli, divided into florets and stalks overtop.

In a saucepan combine the white sauce, stock and tarragon; boil down to half. Add the vermouth or wine and cream, nutmeg, salt and pepper to taste. Remove from heat. The sauce should have a moderately thick consistency. Add the cheese gradually to the sauce and then pour the sauce over the chicken and broccoli. Sprinkle the breadcrumbs over the top. Melt the butter and drizzle over breadcrumbs.

Bake in a 400°F (200°C) oven until the gratin bubbles at the edges and the chicken has heated through.

Variation: Vegetarian Broccoli Gratin

Substitute 2 cups egg noodles, cooked, for the chicken.

Medium White Sauce

(Makes 2 cups)

Ingredients

4	tablespoons butter	2	cups milk
4	tabespoons all-purpose flour		

Method

Melt butter over low heat. Add the flour, stirring, 3–4 minutes or until well blended. Slowly stir in the milk. Simmer and stir the sauce with a wire whisk until it thickens and is smooth and hot.

Chinese Chicken Salad with Grapes

As a change from the garden variety chicken salad, try this one. The combination of flavors provides a new taste experience. Perfect for those light lunches that accompany summer afternoon gatherings. (Serves 4-6)

Ingredients

4 cups chicken, cooked and shredded	2 cups imported red or green grapes, halved or whole and seeded
1 head lettuce, thinly shredded	Lemon dressing (see below)
4 green onions, thinly sliced	3 cups cooked white rice
1 bunch cilantro, chopped (reserve a few leaves for garnish)	1 carrot, thinly sliced on the diagonal
¼ cup sesame seeds, toasted	Additional whole nuts (optional)
1 cup chopped peanuts or slivered almonds	Small clusters of grapes

Method

Mix together the chicken, lettuce, green onions, chopped cilantro, sesame seeds, nuts, and grapes. Pour lemon dressing over the mixture and toss to coat completely. Form a nest of rice on 4–6 individual serving plates. Spoon the chicken mixture over rice and garnish with reserved cilantro leaves, a few carrot slices and additional nuts, if desired. Place small clusters of grapes on each plate alongside the salads.

Lemon Dressing

Ingredients

½ teaspoon dry mustard	1 clove garlic, minced
1 teaspoon sugar	1 teaspoon soy sauce
3 tablespoons lemon juice	¼ cup sesame oil or salad oil

Method

Blend all of the ingredients together well and spoon over salad to taste.

Chicken Livers with Onions and Mint

Mint and vinegar combine to give a fresh, exciting taste to this liver and onion dish. Though the blend of mint and vinegar may sound strange, it is a typical Middle Eastern use for this aromatic herb—and quite delicious. With this combination, there is no need for salt or other seasonings. (Serves 4)

Ingredients

1	pound (500 g) chicken livers
	Freshly ground black pepper
2	tablespoons vegetable oil (corn, safflower, sunflower or other pure vegetable oil)
2	medium onions, thinly sliced
2	cloves garlic
1	tablespoon dried mint or 2

	tablespoons fresh mint, chopped
2	teaspoons flour
5	tablespoons vinegar or lemon juice
2	tablespoons water
2	scallions, chopped

Method

Clean the livers, cut in half and sprinkle with pepper. Dry thoroughly. Heat a large sauté pan and add oil and liver. Sauté the liver for 2–3 minutes on each side until brown. Remove to a plate.

Add the onions to the pan and sauté until soft. Add garlic and soften for 2 or 3 minutes. Add mint and flour and stir to blend, then add lemon juice or vinegar and water. Bring to the boil, stirring to remove anything adhering to the bottom of the pan. Allow to simmer for 2 minutes. Add liver, cover and continue to simmer for 3 minutes more. Top with chopped scallions and serve with tomato rice.

Turkey-in-a-Crust

A simple "one-pot meal" and the perfect answer to what to do with the leftover turkey from the holiday dinner. Served with a fresh green salad, you have a well-balanced and tasty dinner the whole family will enjoy. (Serves 6-8)

Ingredients

	Pastry for a 12" x 9" casserole (single or double crust, as preferred)	¼	cup green onion, minced
		⅓	cup light rum
1	cup shredded Cheddar cheese	1	tablespoon lemon juice
1	tablespoon flour	1	cup mayonnaise
1	cup toasted slivered almonds	½	teaspoon poultry seasoning
3	cups cubed turkey or chicken	½	teaspoon salt
1	cup celery, sliced	⅛	teaspoon pepper
½	cup carrots, sliced		

Method

Roll out the pastry on a lightly floured board to fit a 12 inch x 9 inch casserole. Fit the pastry into dish and scallop edges. Set aside.

Combine ¾ cup of the cheese with the flour, ½ cup almonds, turkey, celery, carrots, green onion, rum, lemon juice, mayonnaise, poultry seasoning, salt and pepper. Spoon into the prepared crust. Top with the remaining cheese and almonds. Bake at 400°F (200°C) for 30 minutes or until the top is golden and the filling is hot.

Glazed Roast Breast of Turkey

This is a perfect meal for small family gatherings, dinner parties, or as a welcome variation to the weekly menus of larger families. Easy to prepare, easy to digest and delicious! (Serves 6)

Ingredients

1	whole turkey breast	Melted butter
	Salt	Cherry glaze

Method

If frozen, thaw the turkey breast in refrigerator several hours or in a pan of cold water 3-4 hours. Wipe the meat with damp paper towels and sprinkle with salt. The breast may be cut in half. If cut in half, cut off the extra flaps of skin and drape over spots where the flesh is exposed. Brush generously with melted butter, top with a loose tent of foil, and roast at 325°F (160°C) about 1½ hours. From then on baste with pan drippings every half hour or so, until the meat is browned and thoroughly tender. Total oven time for either a whole or half breast will take from 3–3½ hours, or until the meat thermometer registers 180-185°F (80-85°C). When done, pour off the pan drippings and save them to make gravy for use with leftovers. Glaze the browned surface of the breast with cherry glaze (see below).

Cherry Glaze

Ingredients

¼	cup dry red wine	1	tablespoon lime or lemon juice
¼	cup drained cherry juice	⅛	teaspoon salt
¼	cup currant jelly	1	cup canned pitted cherries

Method

Heat wine and cherry juice to simmering; add jelly and stir until melted. Remove from heat and add lemon juice, salt and cherries.

Oven Baked Turkey Drumsticks

Why cook a whole turkey when everybody in the family wants the drumstick? Buy turkey drumsticks, bake them, tie them like a crown roast and put the dressing in the middle. Delicious—and no leftovers! (Serves 6)

Ingredients

6	turkey drumsticks	Pepper
	Vegetable oil for brushing (safflower, sunflower, corn or other pure vegetable oil)	¼ teaspoon lemon juice
		3 tablespoons water
	Salt	Favorite dressing

Method

Place the drumsticks in an uncovered pan just large enough to hold them flat. Brush with oil. Bake at 400°F (200°C) for 1 hour, turning often so that they will brown completely. Add salt, pepper, lemon juice and water. Cover with a low tent of heavy aluminum foil, crimping the edges lightly to top edge of pan. Cook until fork tender, about 1¼ hours. The pan drippings may be used for gravy. Remove the large tendons before serving.

To serve as a crown roast, place the drumsticks upright, bone tips in a circle. If necessary, use a heavy needle and twine and sew through the meaty portion of the drumsticks. Cover the tips of the bones with paper frills and fill the centre with the dressing of your choice. Garnish with spiced crabapples and parsley, if desired.

FISH

Fettucine with Mussels and Tomato Sauce

This dish will please even the most fastidious gourmet palate. (Serves 6)

Ingredients

4½	pounds (2.25 kg) fresh mussels	1	bay leaf
2	tablespoons olive oil	1	pound (500 g) fresh or packaged fettucine
1	medium onion, chopped		Salt
3	cloves garlic, chopped	½	cup chopped Italian flat-leaf parsley
½	teaspoon red pepper flakes		
1	teaspoon dried basil		
2	28-ounce (796 mL) cans plum tomatoes, liquid drained (save liquid for Bloody Marys)		

Method

Rinse mussels. Remove hairs and anything that is attached. To test for freshness, try to move the two halves of the shell sideways. If they slide or remain open, throw them out. This means that the mussel is dead, or at best ready to give up the ghost. A strong, lively mussel will hold the shells tightly together. Once washed, store them in the refrigerator in a bowl covered with a damp cloth.

Heat the oil in a heavy 2-quart saucepan and add onion. Stir to soften for about ten minutes over medium-low heat. Onion should not brown. Add the garlic and stir to soften. Add all the remaining ingredients, including the tomatoes and bay leaf. Heat the mixture to a boil, reduce the heat to simmer, covered, for half an hour. Crush the tomatoes as the sauce simmers. Simmer uncovered for 15 minutes or until sauce is desired thickness. Remove bay leaf. Purée the sauce using a food mill, blender or food processor. This sauce will keep refrigerated for 3 days.

About 8 minutes before serving, heat a large pot of water to boiling. Add salt. Drop the fettucine into the boiling water.

Heat a large platter with boiling water or in a low oven. Heat the sauce to boiling. Add the cleaned and rinsed mussels in their shells to the sauce. Cover the sauce and steam the mussels for about 5-7 minutes, or until the mussels open.

Test the pasta by biting it. It should be crisp-tender. Drain the pasta well in a colander to remove any excess water. Transfer to the warmed platter. Top with mussels (shells and all) and sauce and scatter parsley overtop.

Italian cooks *never* serve cheese with fish. If you are a gourmet with eclectic tastes, pass freshly grated Parmesan cheese.

Fish in Spicy Sauce

The mellow, spicy flavor of the sauce, along with the crisp texture of the vegetables, complements the mildness of the fish superbly. We serve this Chinese-style dish at the table, surrounded by a bed of steamed, fluffy rice. (Serves 2)

Ingredients

8	dried Chinese mushrooms	2	tablespoons dry sherry
1	5-ounce (142 g) can water chestnuts, rinsed in boiling water, drained and sliced	1	tablespoon light flavored soy sauce
4	medium green onions, greens and white bulb trimmed and sliced	2	teaspoons sesame oil
		1	teaspoon chili paste
		$1/4$	teaspoon sugar
2	cloves garlic, peeled and chopped	$1/2$	cup cornstarch
		$1^1/_2$	tablespoons cold water
1	slice (about $1/4$ inch) fresh ginger, peeled and slivered	2	whole trout, about 1-1¼ pounds (500-625 g) total
2	teaspoons orange zest	5	tablespoons vegetable oil
$3/4$	cup orange juice or chicken stock		Hot, cooked rice

Method

Put the dried mushrooms in a small bowl, cover with warm water and set aside to soak until soft, about 20 minutes. Drain. Cut off and discard the stems. Cut the mushrooms into bite-size pieces. Set aside in a large bowl with water chestnuts and green onions.

Combine chopped garlic, slivered ginger and orange zest in a small bowl and set aside.

Stir together the orange juice or chicken stock, sherry, soy sauce, sesame oil, chili paste and sugar. Set aside.

Stir together 1 tablespoon of the cornstarch with the water. Set aside.

Put the remaining cornstarch in a large plastic bag. Dip the trout in the cornstarch to coat; shake off the excess.

Heat a large cast-iron skillet or wok until very hot. Add the oil, tilting the pan to cover the surface. When the oil is very hot, add the trout. Cook for about 3 minutes on each side, checking often to keep the skin from sticking. Remove and drain on paper towels. Keep hot on a warmed plate in a warm oven.

Discard all but 1 tablespoon of the oil from the skillet or wok. Add the reserved garlic mixture and cook over moderate heat for about 10 seconds without letting the garlic brown. Add the reserved mushrooms, water chestnuts and green onions and stir for about 10 seconds. Add the reserved sherry mixture. Bring to a boil. Stir in the reserved cornstarch liquid to thicken the sauce slightly.

Return the trout to the skillet for about 30 seconds or until heated through, turning once. Taste the sauce and adjust with sugar, salt or pepper as needed. With a slotted spatula remove the trout to heated plates. Pour the sauce over the top and serve with hot cooked rice.

Fillet of Fish with Tangerines

Combining fish and citrus is always interesting. I've made this dish with grapefruit, tangelos, and even tiny Spanish oranges. If tangerines are un-available, try any of the others. (Serves 4)

Ingredients

2	pounds (1 kg) skinless, boneless fillets of firm-fleshed fish such as cod or red snapper	4	tangerines
1	teaspoon ground coriander	2	tablespoons vegetable oil (corn, safflower, sunflower, or other pure vegetable oil)
½	cup fresh orange or grapefruit juice	2	tablespoons lemon juice
	Salt	4	tablespoons butter
	Freshly ground black pepper	2	tablespoons chopped parsley

Method

Preheat the broiler to high. Cut each fillet crosswise in half. Arrange the fish halves close together in one layer in a rimmed dish. Marinate the fish in coriander, fruit juice, salt and pepper for 10–15 minutes. Meanwhile, peel and section the tangerines. Set aside.

Drain the fish fillets, saving the marinade. Arrange the fish on a baking sheet and brush with oil to coat evenly on both sides. Sprinkle with salt and pepper and place under the broiler about 4 inches from the source of heat. Leave the broiler door slightly open. Broil the fish for 10-12 minutes. Turn halfway through broiling time if the fish is thicker than one inch. Baste with oil if turning.

Meanwhile, bring the marinade and lemon juice to the boil in a sauté or frying pan. While boiling, add the butter using a whisk to incorporate it. Add the tangerines and heat

Remove the fish to heated plates or a platter, spoon over the sauce and tangerines. Sprinkle with parsley and serve.

Lobster Crêpe Supreme

Crab, shrimp, clams, oysters, salmon or tuna may be substituted for the lobster in this very elegant dish. It can be made ahead and frozen, ready for its final baking at party-time. (Makes 12 crêpes)

Ingredients

1	11.3-ounce (320 g) can lobster meat	1	cup milk
¼	cup butter	1	cup dry white wine
¼	cup chopped green onion	1	tablespoon lemon juice
¼	cup minced green pepper	1	teaspoon salt
1	cup minced mushrooms	¼	teaspoon pepper
¼	cup flour	½	teaspoon dried dill weed
		12	crêpes

Method

Cut or break lobster meat into bite-size pieces. Melt butter in a saucepan and sauté the green onion, green pepper and mushrooms for 2 minutes. Stir in the flour, then slowly add milk, stirring constantly over medium heat until thickened. Add the wine, lemon juice, salt, pepper, dill and lobster. Remove from heat.

Spoon 3 tablespoons of this filling onto each crêpe and roll up, folding down the ends so that the filling is contained. Arrange filled crêpes in a lightly greased, shallow oven dish and cover.

Heat oven to 350°F (180°C) and bake filled crêpes for 10–15 minutes, until heated through. If desired, heat the remaining filling, thinned as necessary with milk or sour cream, and serve in a separate dish to spoon over the crêpes.

Reprinted courtesy of *The Canadian Fish Cookbook*, A. Jan Howarth, Douglas & McIntyre, 1984.

Tuna and Grape Salad

(Serves 4)

Ingredients

1	6-ounce (170 mL) jar marinated artichoke hearts		Shredded crisp lettuce
1	cup green, red or black grape halves	1	8-ounce (198 g) can solid white tuna, drained
	Lettuce leaves	¼	cup crumbled Feta cheese

Method

Drain artichoke hearts; reserve marinade. Slice grapes in half and remove any seeds. Line 4 individual salad plates with small lettuce leaves. Top each with shredded lettuce. Arrange grapes, artichoke hearts (cut larger ones in half) and tuna on lettuce. Sprinkle with cheese. Serve with Lemon Herb Dressing (following).

Lemon Herb Dressing
(Makes ¾ cup dressing)

Ingredients

	Marinade from artichoke hearts	½	teaspoon onion salt (optional)
	Vegetable oil	½	teaspoon crushed basil
⅓	cup lemon juice	⅛	teaspoon grated lemon peel
1	tablespoon Dijon mustard	⅛	teaspoon pepper
1	tablespoon honey	⅛	teaspoon fresh garlic, chopped or mashed

Method

Pour marinade from artichoke hearts into measuring cup and add oil to measure ½ cup. Add all the remaining ingredients and blend well. Let stand an hour or longer to mix flavors.

Salmon Supper Cakes
(Serves 4)

Ingredients

2	7¾-ounce (220 g) cans salmon	1	green onion, chopped
2	eggs	1½	cups grated raw potato*
½	teaspoon paprika		Butter or vegetable oil
½	teaspoon dry mustard		

Method

Flake salmon, along with its juices and well-mashed bones, into a mixing bowl. Add the remaining ingredients and mix well. Form into eight patties. Fry on both sides in a small amount of butter or oil until nicely browned. Serve with Yogurt Sauce (following) and accompany with green beans and cabbage salad.

---

*1½ cups cold mashed potatoes or 1 cup instant mashed potato flakes may be substituted.

Yogurt Sauce

Ingredients

1	cup unflavored yogurt	¼	teaspoon dill weed
½	cup milk		Dash Tabasco

Method

Combine all ingredients and pour into the frying pan after removing salmon cakes. Heat gently *just* until warmed through. Serve immediately.

Baked Salmon
(Serves 4)

Ingredients

1	7¾-ounce (220 g) can salmon		Salt
1	cup cooked rice		Pepper
¼	cup sliced ripe olives	1	egg yolk
2	tablespoons minced green onion	2	egg whites
¼	cup lemon juice	1	tablespoon melted butter (optional)

Method

Prepare 4 custard cups first, buttered and coated lightly with fine bread-crumbs.

Drain salmon, reserving 2 tablespoons of liquid. Mix the salmon, reserved liquid, rice, olives, onion, lemon juice, salt, pepper and egg yolk. Beat the egg whites until stiff and fold into the salmon mixture. Spoon into prepared custard cups and brush with melted butter, if desired. Bake in a preheated 375°F (190°C) oven for 30 minutes.

Mom's Creamed Salmon
(Serves 3-4)

Ingredients

3	tablespoons butter	1	7¾-ounce (220 g) can salmon
3	tablespoons flour	½	cup frozen peas
1½	cups milk	½	teaspoon Worcestershire sauce

Method

Melt butter in a medium-sized saucepan. Stir in flour. Slowly add milk a little at a time, stirring constantly to prevent lumping. Add salmon juices and salmon, broken into chunks. Run some hot water over the frozen peas to take the chill off. Add along with Worcestershire sauce. Cook until heated through. Serve immediately over toast, rice, pasta or potato pancakes.

Microwave Method

Place butter and flour in medium-sized glass mixing bowl. Microwave for 45 seconds or until butter is melted; stir to mix. Add milk slowly, stirring constantly. Microwave on high for about 3 minutes, stirring every minute, until mixture has bubbled and thickened. Add chunked salmon, salmon juices, peas and Worcestershire. Return to microwave for one minute or until heated through.

Shrimp and Peas

(Serves 3-4)

Ingredients

1	pound (500 g) raw shrimp, shelled and deveined	½	cup water chestnuts, sliced
1	tablespoon rice wine or sherry	1	cup chicken stock
3	tablespoons peanut oil or a light vegetable oil	2	tablespoons cornstarch
½	teaspoon diced red chilies	4	tablespoons water
1	clove garlic, chopped	¾	teaspoon sesame oil
1½	teaspoons chopped ginger root		
½	pound (250 g) fresh (shelled) or frozen peas		

Method

Cut shrimp in half (slit down back), and cut into ½-inch pieces. Add rice wine or sherry to shrimp and toss.

Heat wok. Add oil, dried chilies, garlic and ginger root. Sauté for 30 seconds. Add shrimp and sauté 2 minutes (until pink). Add peas and stir-fry for 2 minutes. Add water chestnuts and stock. Bring to boil. Mix cornstarch with water and add. Cook until thickened.

Just before serving, drizzle with sesame oil and toss to coat shrimp. Serve on steaming rice.

Sweet and Sour Sole
(Serves 2-3)

Ingredients

1	16-ounce (454 g) box frozen sole	¾	cup cold water
3	tablespoons vegetable oil	¼	cup cucumber, washed, quartered lengthwise and finely sliced
2	cloves garlic, finely chopped		
3	tablespoons vinegar	3	green onions, sliced
5	tablespoons sugar	1	tablespoon diced ginger root
2	teaspoons soy sauce		
⅛	teaspoon pepper		Peel of 1 lemon, cut in fine slivers
1	tablespoon cornstarch dissolved in	6–8	cherry tomatoes, quartered

Method

Sauté sole fillets in vegetable oil for 7 minutes, turning once. Set aside on a warm platter and keep warm. Brown the garlic in pan until golden and add the vinegar, sugar, soy sauce, and pepper. Add the cornstarch with cold water and bring to a boil. Add cucumber, onions, ginger and lemon. Cook covered for 4 minutes. Add tomatoes and continue cooking for one minute more. Pour over the fish. Serve with steamed rice, seasoned with parsley.

Salmon Grapefruit Salad

A light, tangy, easy-to-make salad with crunchy bits of celery and walnuts. (Serves 6)

Ingredients

3	small grapefruit, halved	¾	cup chopped celery
2	7¾-ounce (220 g) cans salmon	¼	cup coarsely chopped walnuts

Method

Using a grapefruit knife, carefully remove fruit from grapefruit halves. Cut the fruit into segments, removing all the membrane. Scrape the shells clean and set aside. Drain salmon, reseving juices for Green Onion Dressing (see below). Break the salmon into chunks. Gently toss grapefruit segments, salmon, celery, and nuts together. Spoon into grapefruit shells. Cover with plastic wrap and chill thoroughly before serving with dressing on the side.

Green Onion Dressing

(Makes 1¼ cups)

Ingredients

	Reserved salmon juices	1	teaspoon Worcestershire sauce
½	cup creamed cottage cheese	¼	teaspoon garlic powder
¼	cup plain yogurt	½	teaspoon Dijon mustard
4	sprigs parsley	¼	cup mayonnaise
1	green onion, chopped	½	teaspoon sugar

Method

Place all ingredients in blender jar and blend until smooth. Refrigerate until ready to serve.

MEATLESS MAIN DISHES

Herbed Egg Salad Ring
(Serves 8)

Ingredients

1	tablespoon unflavored gelatin	1¾	cups mayonnaise, *or*
½	cup cold water	1	cup mayonnaise with
8	large, hard-cooked eggs, chilled, shelled	¾	cup yogurt
		1	teaspoon Dijon mustard
1	cup parsley leaves, minced	1	teaspoon basil, chopped
6	scallions, both green and white parts, finely minced	1	teaspoon dill, chopped
		1	teaspoon savoury, chopped
2	small zucchini, trimmed, peeled and finely minced	¼	teaspoon thyme, chopped
		¼	teaspoon curry powder
1	medium cucumber, unpeeled, halved, coarsely chopped	⅛	teaspoon Tabasco or other hot pepper sauce
1	small clove garlic, peeled and finely chopped		Lettuce, watercress

Method

Oil a 5 or 6-cup mould or use 8 individual moulds.

In a cup, soften gelatin in cold water. Place cup in a pot containing hot water until the gelatin is dissolved (or place it in a microwave oven, uncovered, for 1 minute at a low setting). Set aside.

Coarsely chop eggs in a large mixing bowl and add parsley, scallions, zucchini and cucumber.

In another bowl combine garlic, mayonnaise, mustard and seasonings. Add gelatin and blend.

Add the mayonnaise mixture to the chopped eggs and vegetables; mix well. Adjust seasoning if desired.

Spoon the egg mixture into the ring mould or individual moulds, distributing the mixture evenly. Cover with plastic wrap and refrigerate at least 4 hours until firm.

Basil Almond Stuffed Eggs
(Makes 12 stuffed eggs)

Ingredients

6	hard-boiled eggs, halved	1½	teaspoons Dijon mustard
⅓	cup sour cream or yogurt	½	teaspoon paprika
¼	cup firmly packed fresh basil leaves, minced		Salt to taste
¼	cup almonds, blanched, toasted, finely chopped		Pepper to taste

Method

Remove the egg yolks and arrange whites on a plate lined with paper towels. Force the yolks through a sieve into a bowl. Add sour cream or yogurt, basil, almonds, mustard, paprika, and salt and pepper, if desired. Blend the mixture well. Chill the mixture, covered, for 1 hour. Transfer the mixture to a pastry bag fitted with a medium plain tip and pipe it into the whites. Arrange the stuffed eggs on a serving dish.

Basic Soufflé

A basic soufflé is like a basic black dress: a few simple accessories and it can go anywhere! (Serves 4)

Ingredients

1	tablespoon butter	1	cup warm milk
1	tablespoon fine bread-crumbs or freshly grated Parmesan cheese	4	egg yolks
		½	teaspoon salt
3	tablespoons butter		Cayenne pepper
3	tablespoons flour	6–7	egg whites
		¼	teaspoon cream of tartar

Suggested Flavorings

Ingredients

1   cup grated cheese
½   teaspoon dry mustard

½   cup finely chopped, cooked chicken
⅓   cup chopped mushrooms
1   teaspoon parsley

⅓   cup liqueur
4   tablespoons sugar (omit salt
    from basic recipe)

Method

Butter a 1½ quart straight-sided soufflé dish and coat the inside surface evenly with breadcrumbs or cheese. Refrigerate the dish for at least 30 minutes.

Place butter in a heavy saucepan and melt over low heat. Remove. Add the flour and stir vigorously with a whisk until the mixture is smooth. Pour in the milk gradually. Beat, using a whisk until well combined. Place the pan over high heat and, whisking constantly, bring the sauce to a boil. When it is thick and smooth, lower heat. Stirring frequently, cook slowly for 1 or 2 minutes. Remove the pan from the heat.

Quickly whisk the egg yolks one at a time. Add any one of the flavorings. Mix thoroughly with a wooden spoon or whisk until the sauce is smooth. Taste the sauce for seasoning. Remember that a soufflé base should be slightly overseasoned if the soufflé is to have any character when the beaten egg whites are added. Cover with plastic wrap and set aside.

Just before baking and serving, prepare oven. Place oven shelf into the centre of the oven and preheat at 400°F (200°C) for 15 minutes.

Put the egg whites in the bowl of your electric mixer or, if you are using a rotary beater or a large whisk, in a large glass, stainless-steel, or copper bowl. Beat lightly until foamy. Add cream of tartar. Continue beating until whites form firm, glossy peaks.

Using a wire whisk, vigorously beat about a cup of the whites into the soufflé base. Then, with a rubber spatula, reverse the process and scrape the soufflé base over the remaining whites. Gently combine them, using the spatula to cut and fold the mixture each quarter turn as you rotate the bowl in a full circle. Fold gently just until no streaks of egg white show.

Pour the soufflé mixture into the prepared dish and place the dish in the centre of the oven. Immediately turn the heat down to 375°F (190°C) and bake for 25–30 minutes, or until the soufflé has puffed above the dish and browned lightly. For a firm rather than a creamy centre, bake the soufflé an additional 5 minutes. Serve at once.

Pasta Primavera

(Serves 6)

Ingredients

1	pound (454 g) spaghetti or other long pasta
1	cup zucchini, sliced
1½	cups broccoli, broken into florets
1½	cups snow peas (optional)
1	cup baby peas
6	stalks asparagus, sliced
1	tablespoon vegetable oil (corn, safflower, sunflower or other pure vegetable oil)
12	cherry tomatoes cut in half

1	clove garlic, minced
¼	cup Italian flat-leaf parsley, chopped
	Salt and pepper to taste
⅓	cup pine nuts
10	large mushrooms, sliced
1	teaspoon minced garlic
⅓	cup butter
½	cup Parmesan cheese
½	cup 18% cream
⅓	cup fresh chopped basil
	Parmesan cheese for passing

Method

Blanch the zucchini, broccoli, snow peas, baby peas and asparagus in boiling water for 1–2 minutes until just crisp-tender. Rinse in a bowl of ice water. Drain. Set aside.

Heat oil in a large pan and sauté tomatoes with garlic, parsley, salt, and pepper. Remove from pan and set aside.

Using the same pan, sauté pine nuts until light brown in color. Add the pine nuts to the tomato mixture. Reserve. Sauté mushrooms in pan. Put all of the vegetables (except tomatoes) back into sauté pan. Add more garlic if desired. Simmer a few minutes until hot.

While the vegetables are simmering, heat butter in a saucepan. Add cheese and cream. Stir until thickened and add basil. If the sauce is too thick, thin with more cream. Keep warm.

Cook pasta in a large pot of boiling water about 8–10 minutes—until al dente—and drain. Toss the pasta with the cheese/basil sauce. Add ⅓ of the vegetables and toss. Transfer the pasta to a heated platter and top with remaining hot vegetable mixture.

Garnish with the sautéed cherry tomatoes, garlic, parsley and pine nuts. Pass freshly grated Parmesan cheese.

Risotto Primavera

Risotto is one of those dishes that must be prepared just before serving. Standing over a bubbling cauldron of golden-yellow rice, watching it change color is just one of the rewards of such caretaking. It is usually made with boiling chicken stock; here it's made with a vegetable broth served with lightly sautéed vegetables. (Serves 4 as a first course, 2 as a main course)

Ingredients

4 tablespoons vegetable oil	2 cloves garlic, peeled and finely chopped
2 tablespoons finely chopped onion	1 large zucchini, cut in julienne strips
1⅓ cups Arborio rice	4 stalks asparagus, cut in julienne strips
3 cups unsalted vegetable stock, heated to a simmer	
½ teaspoon salt (optional)	1 tablespoon each, chopped fresh basil and parsley
⅓ cup grated Parmesan cheese	Black pepper to taste
10 fresh mushrooms, sliced	
1 red pepper, cut in julienne strips	

Method

Heat 2 tablespoons of the oil in a heavy saucepan and cook the onion over moderate heat just until translucent. Stir in the rice and cook it a minute or two, coating it thoroughly with the oil. Add a ladleful of stock, and the salt. Bring the mixture to a boil, then reduce the heat to a lively simmer. Cook the rice stirring it frequently to prevent sticking and to scrape down any grains sticking to the side of the pot, until the liquid is nearly absorbed. Add another ladleful of stock, stir, and cook until this is absorbed. The cooking process will take about 10-15 minutes altogether. Test the rice by biting a single grain. If the centre is still raw, add another ladleful of stock, and cook until it is absorbed. Test the rice again. The goal is to have the last bit of stock absorbed when the outside of each grain is tender and creamy and the centre is firm, like pasta cooked *al dente*.

Toss the rice with the grated cheese. Taste and add salt, if necessary. As the rice is finished cooking, heat the remaining oil in a skillet and sauté the mushrooms, pepper and garlic until the pepper begins to soften. Add zucchini, asparagus and herbs. Remove the pan from the heat, cover and set aside. Five minutes before the risotto is done, stir in the vegetables. Serve immediately.

Julie Dannenbaum's Noodle Mould
(Serves 8-10)

Ingredients

11 lasagna noodles, cooked and drained
Melted butter
1 10½-ounce (284 mL) can cream of mushroom soup
4 eggs, lightly beaten
¼ cup milk

1 cup Ricotta or cottage cheese
¾ cup grated Parmesan cheese
½ cup chopped fresh parsley
1 teaspoon basil
3 cups cooked fine noodles
Cooked green beans or other vegetable

Method

Butter hot lasagna noodles. Arrange the noodles crosswise in the bottom of a well-buttered 6-cup ring mould. Let the ends hang loose over the sides of the mould. Mix the soup, eggs, milk, cheeses, parsley and basil. Add fine noodles and stir to mix thoroughly. Pour into noodle-lined mould. Fold the ends of the lasagne noodles over top of filling, trimming any excess. Brush generously with melted butter. Bake at 350°F (180°C) for 45 minutes.

Remove from oven and let stand for 10 minutes. Carefully loosen from sides with a knife. Unmould onto serving plate. Fill the centre with cooked green beans.

Curried Zucchini Pilaf with Pineapple

Curry powder, with its cumin and coriander, is nicely balanced by pineapple. The contrasting flavors are delicious without any additional salt or sugar. (Serves 4-6)

Ingredients

2 cups cooked white or brown rice
2 tablespoons lemon juice
¼ cup chopped parsley
¾ cup pineapple, chopped into ½-inch cubes
3 tablespoons vegetable oil
1 cup chopped onion

2 bay leaves
1 teaspoon grated fresh ginger
2 teaspoons curry powder
2 medium zucchini, scrubbed clean and cut into ½-inch cubes
Roasted peanuts or pine nuts, chopped, for garnish (optional)

Method

Mix rice, lemon juice, parsley and pineapple in a bowl. Set aside. Heat oil in a two-quart saucepan over high heat for 2 minutes. Add onion and cook, stirring, for 3–4 minutes or until onion looks wilted and slightly browned. Add bay leaves and ginger and continue cooking for 1 minute longer. Sprinkle curry powder over the onion and cook, stirring constantly, until it loses the raw smell, about 2 minutes. Add zucchini and stir-fry for about 2 minutes, or until the vegetables begin to turn limp. Cover, lower heat, and cook for 5 minutes.

Uncover, add rice mixture, and continue cooking, covered, for an additional 5–8 minutes or until the vegetables are fully cooked and the rice is thoroughly heated. (If the rice looks very dry, add 3–4 tablespoons of water when adding the rice to vegetables.) Uncover, fluff the pilaf and transfer to serving platter. Sprinkle with chopped roasted peanuts or pine nuts, if desired.

Serve as a main dish with sliced cucumbers in yogurt and chopped mint.

Sweet Baked Beans
(Serves 2-3)

Ingredients

½ cup raisins	1½ teaspoons dry mustard
1 small onion	¼ cup sweet pickle relish
1 tart apple	½ cup ketchup or chili sauce
½ cup chopped ham	
1 28-ounce (796 mL) can baked beans	

Method

Finely chop or coarsely grind the raisins, onion and apple. Combine all ingredients. Turn into a saucepan and cook over moderate temperature until heated through.

Spanakopita

Spinach and cheese casseroles originate in many cultures: the combinations foretell their roots. Sephardic Jews use mild hard cheese, cottage cheese and sesame seeds; Italians use Ricotta, Parmesan cheese and pine nuts; Greek cooks combine spinach with Feta cheese and dill weed. We've given you the Greek version, but whichever combination you prefer, the choice wrapping is filo pastry. (Serves 6)

Ingredients

14 sheets filo pastry (see pp. 74–78)

½ cup clarified butter

2 pounds (1 kg) fresh spinach with stems removed, *or*

2 10-ounce (300 g) packages frozen chopped spinach, defrosted

3 tablespoons olive oil

4 green onions, chopped (including green tops)

½ pound Feta cheese

2 large cloves garlic, minced

1½ teaspoons dill weed, fresh if possible

Freshly ground pepper to taste

Method

If you are using fresh spinach, wash and dry it thoroughly. If you are using frozen spinach, let it drain thoroughly in a colander, squeezing out the excess moisture by pressing with a large spoon.

In a large pot, heat the olive oil. Add the green onions and spinach and cook, stirring constantly until the spinach wilts. This takes just a few minutes. Place in a colander and let drain completely for at least 1 hour. Set aside.

In a separate bowl, crumble the Feta cheese. Mix in the garlic, dill weed and pepper, then add the drained spinach.

Prepare filo or use prepared sheets. If the pastry is frozen, thaw it completely or it will be too brittle to use.

Line a 9 inch x 13 inch buttered baking pan crosswise with 8 layers of filo, brushing clarified butter between each piece. Let the extra dough hang over the side. Put in the cooled filling and bring the extra dough over it. Lay 6 more sheets of filo overtop, brushing butter between each sheet. Tuck under the sides. Bake at 400°F (200°C) for 15 minutes, then reduce heat to 375°F (190°C) for 20 minutes longer. Serve hot.

Baked Potato Surprise

A nourishing, comforting main course for those nights when nothing much is happening, it's snowing outside and you have a good book nearby. Plenty of good nutrition and delicious, besides! (Serves 2)

Ingredients

2	large baking potatoes	4	teaspoons prepared mustard
	Vegetable oil for brushing	1	tablespoon unflavored yogurt
2	poached eggs	1	tablespoon milk, or more
1	tablespoon vinegar	2	tablespoons caraway seeds,
1	teaspoon salt		sesame seeds or dill seeds
2	tablespoons chopped green onions		

Method

Preheat toaster or regular oven to 400°F (200°C). Scrub and dry potatoes and rub well with vegetable oil. Prick the skins in several places with a fork to allow steam to escape and bake for 45 minutes to 1 hour—until potatoes are done.

Meanwhile poach eggs. Butter or lightly oil the bottom of a 9-inch skillet. Add cold water to a depth of 2½ inches. Bring to a boil. Add vinegar and salt; lower heat to simmer. Break each egg into a saucer, then slide into the bath of water. Let the eggs cook for 3½ minutes. Using a slotted, flat spoon, remove them to several thicknesses of paper towel. Place the dried poached eggs on a flat, heated plate.

When potatoes are baked, cut a ½-inch slice from the top and carefully scoop out potato into a bowl. Mash the potato pieces thoroughly and mix with all ingredients except seeds. Taste and adjust seasoning.

Fill the potato shells ⅓ full and place a hot poached egg in shell. Top with remaining mixture and drizzle seeds overtop. Place back in the oven and reheat for 10 minutes. Lean back and enjoy!

BREADS AND BAKED SAVORIES

Fruited Oat Bread

An old-fashioned, stick-to-your ribs oat bread that is both filling and sweet. (Makes 1 loaf)

Ingredients

¾	cup milk	½	cup lukewarm water
½	cup quick-cooking rolled oats	1	teaspoon granulated sugar
1	teaspoon salt	1	envelope dry yeast
1	tablespoon granulated sugar	2¾	cups all-purpose flour, approximately
2	tablespoons vegetable oil (corn, safflower, sunflower or other pure vegetable oil)	½	cup seedless raisins
		½	cup cut-up pitted dates
¼	cup molasses		

Method

Scald milk. Stir in rolled oats, salt, the one tablespoon sugar, oil and molasses. Keep lukewarm.

Measure lukewarm water into a large bowl. Stir in the one teaspoon sugar. Sprinkle with yeast. Let stand 10 minutes, then stir well. Stir in lukewarm oat mixture and 1¼ cups of the flour. Beat until smooth and elastic. Mix in dates and raisins. Work in sufficient additional flour to make a soft dough—about 1½ cups more. Turn out the dough onto a floured board or canvas and knead until smooth and elastic. Place in a greased bowl and turn dough to grease all sides. Cover. Let rise in a warm place, free from draft, until doubled in bulk—about 1¼ hours. Punch down dough.

Turn out onto a lightly floured board or canvas and knead until smooth. Shape into a loaf and place in a greased 4½ inch × 8½ inch loaf pan. Grease top. Cover. Let rise in a warm place, free from draft, until doubled in bulk—about 45 minutes. Bake in a preheated oven at 375°F (190°C) for 35–40 minutes.

Braided Challah

Challah is the traditional Sabbath and Jewish Festival bread, braided, glazed and dotted with sesame or poppy seeds. It is served in Jewish homes every Friday evening to celebrate the arrival of the Sabbath and, when braided correctly, will be made with seven strands, one for each day of the week. Because it is soft textured, it is simple to work with and especially delicious to eat. Normally, it is made with white flour only; this version has whole grains and wheat germ to enrich it further. (Makes 1 large loaf or 2 small ones)

Ingredients

¼	cup honey	1	cup whole-wheat flour
1	cup (scant) lukewarm water	¼	cup natural bran
1	tablespoon dry yeast	1	teaspoon wheat germ
2	eggs, lightly mixed (remove 2 tablespoons for glaze)	2	teaspoons salt
½	cup (scant) vegetable oil (corn, safflower, sunflower or other pure vegetable oil)	½	cup sesame or poppy seeds (sesame make a heavier loaf; poppy seeds make a sweeter one)
3	cups all-purpose flour		

Method

Combine the honey and water. Test the temperature of the mixture with your fingers; it should be slightly warmer than body temperature. Sprinkle the yeast over the surface of the water and leave for 15 minutes until the yeast has dissolved. The little pellets will first drop to the bottom, then rise to the surface one by one and explode to create a "head" of puffy foam.

Measure the dry ingredients and blend together. Stir the yeast and liquid and add, along with the eggs and oil, all at once, to the dry ingredients. Work with your hands until all the dry particles are gathered in to form a rough, slightly sticky lump of dough. Turn the dough out onto a clean, dry surface and knead thoroughly. If the dough is too sticky and difficult to handle, work in only enough extra flour to make it manageable. This is unlikely to be necessary. Remember that dough becomes less sticky once the gluten is developed. Knead for not less than 5 minutes, preferably for 10 minutes. When the dough has had sufficient kneading, it will have changed from a sticky mass to a smooth dough that feels elastic, no longer sticks to the board and has many tiny air bubbles under the surface.

To knead, push the part of the dough farthest from you with the heel of the hand, then pull and fold the dough back into the centre with the fingers. Turn the piece of dough by quarters and continue pushing, pulling, folding and turning, so that all of the dough receives equal manipulation.

Grease a straight-sided container, bowl, casserole or measuring cup that holds 4 cups exactly. Place the dough inside, turning it over and around so that the entire surface of the dough is coated with oil. A smooth surface is essential for a uniform bread. Cover the container with plastic wrap and a clean tea towel and allow to rise in a warm place. If the kitchen is cold, use an electric heating pad, lightly wrapped in a towel and set at low, to surround the bowl. The temperature for bread should be no higher than 70°F (21°C), otherwise it tastes yeasty. When the dough mounds up to the top it is ready. This will likely take 1½ hours. If the room temperature is cooler than 70°F (21°C) it will take longer. (If doubling the recipe, a 6-cup container will do.)

The dough is ready when two fingers inserted to the knuckles leave a deep impression. Test at the side rather than the centre of the dough. If it is ready, lightly punch the dough down in the centre to release the air bubbles. Flatten the dough, bring all sides to the centre and form into a ball. Turn over so that the folded ends are on the bottom. Cover again and set aside to rise once more. It takes slightly less time than the first rise (1¼ hours). Test again with the fingers for lightness and proceed to shape.

Turn the dough out onto the board and knead to release any large bubbles that are near the surface. Then round into a ball and separate into 3 lumps of dough for a simple 3-strand braid. Form each piece of dough into lengths 11 or 12 inches long. Do this by pulling and rolling the lump until it forms a coil. Now begin braiding from the centre to each end. For a more complex 7-strand loaf, divide the dough into 4 equal lumps. Braid 3 as described above, to make the basic large loaf. Divide the fourth lump of dough into 4 equal-size strands. Braid 3 and place these on top of the larger loaf. Roll and stretch the fourth strand and weave it through the small and large loaf in an alternate manner.

Be sure that you braid these tightly; there should be no air between any of the strands. Brush the surface with oil.

To bake on a cookie sheet place the braid on an oiled sheet, cover and let rise until it is double in bulk. This should take between 1–1½ hours.

To bake in a loaf pan fit the braided loaf into a lightly greased pan, cover and allow to rise as above.

Brush the remaining egg mixture onto the raised bread and sprinkle with sesame or poppy seeds. Bake at 350°F (180°C) for 10 minutes. Cover with foil and continue baking for 20–30 minutes more. When done place on rack, remove from pan and allow to cool. This loaf will keep for a week, and makes wonderful toast.

Kitchen Machine with Dough Hook Method
Prepare the dough using the ingredients above and following the kneading method in the instruction manual for your machine. *Note: never knead at a speed over 2 or 3 on your machine.* Continue with the same shaping and rising method for hand-kneaded bread.

Food Processor Method
Combine 2½ cups all-purpose flour with the balance of the dry ingredients in the work bowl fitted with the metal blade. Reserve ½ cup flour for later use.

Use ½ cup warm water to dissolve the honey and yeast and keep ½ cup *cold* water for adding later. (The blade travels at such a high speed that it is possible to raise the temperature some degrees more than is good for the yeast.) Process on/off to combine flours and other dry ingredients. Measure the egg and oil and keep handy.

Add the yeast solution to the flour and process on/off quickly. Add cold water and egg and oil mixture through the feed tube and process until the dough forms a ball. If it is too sticky (sticks to sides of bowl), add more flour until it forms a tacky but not glue-like ball of dough. This whole process should take under 60 seconds. Remove the dough, knead for about a minute by hand to smooth the dough and place in a greased bowl to rise. Follow the rising and shaping instructions for hand-kneaded dough above.

Filo and Strudel Pastry
Filo (phyllo, fillo) is a delicate, light, flaky pastry that originated in the Middle East. Filo means "leaf" in Greek; that tells you how very thin it is. Ready-made filo is now available everywhere—in supermarket freezers, in specialty food shops and in bakeries where Middle Eastern food is sold. Filo is used as a wrapper for sweet and savory dishes, to cover everything from liver pâté to a poached fruit dessert. It looks more difficult to prepare than it is and the shapes are limited only by your imagination. The traditional Spanakopita (Greek spinach pie) and apple strudel are popular examples of its adaptability. The food processor makes filo and strudel quite simple to prepare.

Preparation

Allow two hours of uninterrupted time. Filo dries quickly and will not wait during preparation. If for any reason it must be left, cover it with a damp (not wet) towel and refrigerate. Have equipment, filling and ingredients ready.

Equipment

baking sheet
brush
pizza cutter or scissors
sharp knife
spatula
2 damp towels

Working with filo dough

One pound of filo is the amount most often needed for recipes. The number of sheets required for each layer in a recipe varies according to your taste. Try to work on a dry day, out of direct sunlight, away from heat vent. Lay out the filo on a dry cloth in separate sheets and cut to suit recipe. If any pieces tear, lay another sheet over the top and use as one sheet.

Storage and freezing

If your filo has already been frozen once and allowed to defrost, it cannot be frozen a second time. Be sure to check with the store clerk when buying ready-made filo. Allow filo to defrost in the refrigerator 1–2 days so that the sheets will stay dry and separate easily. Filo can be kept in the refrigerator 3–4 weeks unopened; once the package has been opened it will keep an additional 2 weeks, stored in an airtight plastic bag with all the air pressed out of it.

Stuffed pastry can be stored in the refrigerator 2–3 days and can go directly from the refrigerator to the oven for baking.

If you are freezing single sheets, cut them to size, freeze and stack with waxed paper between. Wrap carefully with foil or heavy plastic. If freezing in a baking pan, be sure pan is well-sealed so no air can get in. If freezing individual pastries, place them uncovered on a baking sheet in a single layer in the freezer. Once they become hard, stack in a freezer container, separating layers with sheets of waxed paper. Cover container tightly. Remove from the freezer about 30 minutes to 1 hour (depending on size of the pastry) before baking. Bake frozen pastries slightly longer than time allowed and brush a little extra oil or butter on the pastry while baking.

Homemade filo pastry

There are three keys to successful filo making. First, avoid making it in rainy, humid weather—the damp makes it hard to work with and adds to the time it needs to dry. Secondly, you need a large work table: at least 30 inches wide and free on three sides so you can move easily while working with dough. The table should be covered with a clean, smooth tablecloth or sheet. And thirdly, no jewelry or long sleeves! Rings, watches and buttons tend to snag and tear the filo when you are stretching it. Once secure on these three points, you're ready to go.

Beginner's hint

At first, you may find the stretching process difficult, because you're attempting to stretch the dough over a large surface. It is much simpler, at the beginning, to stretch a smaller piece over a smaller area—the bottom surface of a deep pot, for example. So, instead of cutting the dough into 2 balls, cut it into 4. Then, invert a deep stock pot and cover it with a clean dry towel. Stretch each of the 4 balls of dough over this pan, one at a time, following the instructions given for normal stretching and preparation of the pastry.

Food Processor Filo Pastry

Filo pastry is traditionally prepared with flour, salt and water. Success depends upon the quality of the flour, careful weight and measure, and the temperature of the liquid—it should be warm. (Makes 1 pound—enough for 8 cups filling)

Ingredients

2¼ cups all-purpose flour*	1 teaspoon lemon juice
½ teaspoon salt	½ cup warm water, 105°–115°F
3 tablespoons olive oil	(40°–45°C) (be accurate here!)
1 large egg, warmed in hot water	1 tablespoon sweet butter, melted

---

*To avoid tearing the dough, use a hard wheat, non-blended flour with a high protein content.

Food Processor Strudel Pastry

Strudel and filo pastry are essentially the same. Purchased filo may be substituted for strudel, although it's not *exactly* correct. The main difference between filo and strudel occurs after the dough is rolled out and pulled. Filo is left to dry. Strudel is used right away.

Ingredients

2¼	cups all-purpose flour*	1	teaspoon lemon juice
½	teaspoon sugar	½	cup warm water, 105°–115°F (40°–45°C) (be accurate here!)
½	teaspoon salt		
3	tablespoons vegetable oil (corn, safflower, sunflower or other pure vegetable oil)	1	tablespoon sweet butter, melted
1	large egg, warmed in hot water		

Method

Place flour and dry ingredients into the workbowl fitted with the steel blade; process to combine. Combine oil, egg, lemon juice and ¼ cup warm water in a pitcher or measure; stir to blend and break up egg. With the motor running, add liquid through the feed tube gradually. Add balance of warm water gradually, just until the dough cleans the side of the bowl. There may be 1 tablespoon unused water. This should take from 30–60 seconds. Feel the dough; it should be soft, dry and *slightly* sticky.

Once the ball has formed, process the dough for no more than 45–60 seconds. Check every 15 seconds. The dough, when rounded out of the bowl, should be perfectly smooth. If it is not velvety textured and it has been processed for less than 60 seconds, don't be afraid to return it to the bowl for a further 15 seconds—as long as you do not exceed the 60 seconds total processing time after the dough forms a ball. This processing is the same as old-fashioned kneading. The slapping of the dough against the side of the bowl develops the gluten for stretching. Processing for longer than 1 minute develops too much gluten; the dough will lose elasticity and become stringy and tough.

---

*To avoid tearing the dough, use a hard wheat, non-blended flour with a high protein content.

Remove the dough and form into a ball. Flatten and cut into two balls. Read *beginner's hint* on previous page. Round up each piece of dough by pinching the cut ends together. All the surfaces should be smooth. Brush two plates (four plates) with melted butter. Flatten the balls, place on plates, brush the top surface with butter and cover with plastic wrap. Set in a *warm* place to rest for 30–45 minutes, no longer. To test, touch—it should be soft and offer no resistance. Each ball will weigh ½ pound (¼ pound).

To roll and shape filo and strudel dough
Lay an old sheet or smoth tablecloth over your table and dust the cloth with flour.

At the end of the resting period, place one ball of dough in the middle of the table by sliding it off the plate onto the cloth. Roll out gently with a rolling pin into a 12-inch circle. Pick it up with your fingers and rotate it around on the back of your hands. The dough will stretch under its own weight until it's large enough to drag on the table. At this point, if you are a beginner, try to work with someone more experienced until you get the feel of the dough or follow *beginner's hint*. Lay it on the table and continue stretching with the back of your hands until very thin. When the dough gets large enough, drape over the edges of the table. The edges will remain thick. If an area begins to look puckered, you've stretched it to its limit; avoid any more stretching. Work until the dough looks evenly stretched—each ball will stretch to 36 inches × 42 inches. Let it dry until it no longer feels tacky. Scissor off the thick outer edge. Save trimmings and run them through a pasta machine to make noodles for dinner, if desired.

Chou Pastry
(Makes 12 5-inch eclairs or 15 3-inch cream puffs)

Ingredients

1	cup water	1	cup all-purpose flour
8	tablespoons unsalted butter, cut into pieces	1	teaspoon salt
		4	large eggs

Method

Put the water in a heavy saucepan over medium heat. Add the butter, stirring constantly to help it melt quickly.

Sift the flour and salt onto a piece of waxed paper.

When the butter has melted, increase the heat to bring the water mixture to a boil. Slide the flour off the paper into the water. Stir the mixture until thoroughly combined, then stir over medium heat until the mixture forms a solid mass that comes away cleanly from the sides of the saucepan. Reduce the heat to low and stir constantly for three minutes. Remove the pan from heat and cool the mixture for a few minutes.

Break one egg into a bowl and add it to the contents of the pan, beating with a spoon to incorporate the egg thoroughly. Repeat with the remaining eggs. Continue beating until the ingredients are smoothly blended.

To make pastry for cream puffs

Heat the oven to 400°F (200°C). Cover a buttered baking sheet with parchment paper. Fill a pastry bag with the chou pastry and pipe mounds of it about 1½ inches in diameter onto the paper, spacing the mounds about 1½ inches apart. (Alternatively, you may use a teaspoon to form the mounds of pastry.) Bake in the preheated oven for 15 minutes, or until the pastry has more than doubled in size and is lightly browned and firm to the touch. Pierce each while still in the oven and continue baking 5–7 minutes longer.

To make pastry for éclairs

Heat oven to 400°F (200°C). Cover a buttered baking sheet with parchment paper. Fill a pastry bag with chou pastry and pipe 4-inch strips, about 1½ inches apart, onto the paper. Bake in preheated oven for 15 minutes, or until the pastry is puffed, light brown, and firm to the touch. Pierce each with a sharp knife and continue baking for 5–7 minutes.

Fill with Crème Pâtissière (recipe from What's Cooking, Volume IV, p. 98), sweetened whipped cream or ice cream and top with chocolate glaze.

Irish Soda Bread with Apricots

Always made with buttermilk, flour and soda, an Irish Soda Bread is quick, open textured and crusty. It should be served warm with butter and jam. Ours is fancier, but just as delicious. (Makes 1 round loaf)

Ingredients

4	cups all-purpose flour	¾	cup finely chopped dried apricots
⅓	cup sugar		
1	tablespoon baking powder	1¼	cups dark seedless raisins
1	teaspoon salt	2	teaspoons caraway seeds
¾	teaspoon baking soda	2	slightly beaten eggs
6	tablespoons butter	1½	cups buttermilk

Method

Combine dry ingredients in a large bowl. Cut in butter until mixture resembles coarse crumbs. Stir in apricots, raisins and caraway seeds. Combine eggs with buttermilk and stir into flour mixture just until flour is moistened.

On a well-floured surface, knead dough about 10 times. Shape the dough into a ball; place in a greased 2-quart round casserole. Using a sharp knife or scissors, cut a cross, 4 inches long and ¼ inch deep, in centre of dough. Brush top with melted butter, if desired. Bake at 350°F (180°C) for 1 hour 20 minutes or until toothpick inserted in centre comes out clean. Cool on wire rack 10 minutes; remove bread from casserole. Serve warm.

VEGETABLES, SALADS AND DRESSINGS

Preparing Broccoli

Pick over the broccoli carefully, cutting off the tough ends and any damaged or coarse leaves. For especially fine dishes of broccoli strip off all the leaves, leaving the stalks and heads. Rinse and peel away any hard skin from the stalks.

To steam, tie the broccoli into bundles and stand in a wire basket. In a large saucepan heat 1–2 inches of water to a rolling boil. Put in the basket of broccoli. Sprinkle the tops with salt and pepper, cover, or, if the broccoli tops are above the rim of the pan, cover with another pot, upside down. Steam just until the stalks are tender and the flowering part is bright green, crisp-tender. Remove the basket from the pan and leave it to drain.

Red-Hot Broccoli or Cauliflower

The keys to this dish are a good-flavored oil—olive oil is best—and the chili. If your family isn't used to spicy dishes you may want to start off with only one chili. This recipe is also a great one to spice up cauliflower, a somewhat bland vegetable. Tastes wonderful with scrambled eggs, broiled chicken or fish.

Ingredients

2	pounds (1 kg) broccoli, *or*	½	sweet red pepper, coarsely chopped
1	large cauliflower		Olive oil
2	dried red chilis		

Method

Trim the dead leaves and stringy or tough stalk from the broccoli or cauliflower. Cook the vegetable in boiling water until crisp-tender, about 3 minutes. Immediately plunge in ice water to chill and separate into florets. Cut the broccoli stalks into thin strips.

Chop the chilis and do not discard seeds. Put the chilis, seeds included, and red pepper in a large sauté pan and add enough olive oil to cover the base with a thin layer. Heat gently over low temperature for about 10 minutes to bring the flavor of the chilis into the oil.

Increase the heat to medium and add the broccoli or cauliflower. Stir to reheat and lightly cook the vegetable. Turn several times. Using a slotted spoon, remove the vegetable, chili bits and pepper to a hot dish, making sure to drain off any excess oil. Serve immediately.

Sweet Potatoes Aflame

Sweet pototoes and yams look alike and even, to a certain extent, taste alike, but their botanical description is different since they derive from different plants. The sweet potato is likely American in origin and the yam African. In my experience, a yam's flesh is darker, but each is interchangeable with the other for nutrition and preparation. (Serves 6–8)

Ingredients

6	long sweet potatoes of uniform size	½	cup preserved ginger, liquid drained, sliced thinly
4	large cooking apples	¼	cup butter
1	9¾-ounce (425 mL) can chestnuts, drained		Sugar to taste
		½	cup rum

Method

Parboil potatoes, peel, and cut across into circles about ⅜-inch thick. Core and thinly slice the apples into rings. Fill a deep baking dish with a layer of sweet potatoes, then a layer of apple rings, then chestnuts, then some ginger. Repeat until dish is filled, with a layer of potatoes on top, the circles fitted as closely as possible together. Melt the butter and sugar in a small saucepan, pour over dish and bake in a preheated 350°F (180°C) oven until brown, about 30 minutes. Heat rum, pour over dish immediately before serving and ignite.

Oven Parmesan Chips

No one will believe that these crisp delights are really low calorie. And we won't tell. (Makes 4–6 servings)

Ingredients

4	medium baking potatoes		Pepper
¼	cup butter		Dash paprika
1	tablespoon grated onion	2	tablespoons grated Parmesan cheese
	Salt		

Method

Preheat oven to 425°F (220°C). Wash and cut unpeeled potatoes into ⅛-inch slices and place in a single layer on lightly buttered baking sheets. Melt butter in a small saucepan and add onion, salt, pepper and paprika. Brush butter mixture on potatoes and bake for 15–20 minutes or until potatoes are crisp and golden. Sprinkle with Parmesan cheese and serve at once.

Parsnip Patties

These are wonderful little vegetable cakes to serve at holiday dinners. They are unusual: crusty on the outside, soft and sweet on the inside, and they enhance the flavors of roasted chicken or poultry perfectly. Even nonparsnip eaters love to eat these! (Serves 4)

Ingredients

4	medium parsnips	2	tablespoons milk
2	tablespoons butter	3	tablespoons flour
	Dash pepper	2–3	tablespoons vegetable oil
	Dash garlic powder (if desired)		(corn, safflower, sunflower or other pure vegetable oil)

Method

Wash the parsnips and cook in a little water until tender (about 30 minutes). Drain, cool and peel. Mash thoroughly or whip in the food processor. Add butter, pepper, garlic, if desired, and milk.

Shape into 8 cakes, dip in the flour and brown slowly in the hot oil in a heavy skillet until crisp or brown. These may be drained on paper towel and refrigerated. About 30 minutes before serving, place on a cookie sheet and reheat at 375°F (190°C).

Glazed Parsnips

So good, even dedicated parsnip haters will be won over. (Serves 8)

Ingredients

1	cup water	2	tablespoons brown sugar
2	pounds (1 kg) parsnips, peeled and julienned	¼	cup dark rum
4	tablespoons unsalted butter	1	teaspoon lemon juice
	Freshly ground pepper	2	tablespoons finely chopped fresh parsley
1	sprig fresh rosemary, optional	1	teaspoon salt, optional

Method

In a medium-size sauté pan, bring water, parsnips, butter, and pepper to a boil over high heat. Lower heat to medium, cover, and cook for 5 minutes. Add brown sugar, rum and lemon juice and continue to cook, uncovered, over medium heat for about 8 minutes until almost all liquid has reduced and has become syrupy. Taste, add salt if desired. Add parsley, toss, and serve.

Quick Skillet Succotash
(Makes 4 servings)

Ingredients

4	slices bacon	3	tablespoons butter
2	tablespoons vegetable oil	1	teaspoon dried parsley
1	medium onion		Salt
1	clove garlic, finely chopped		Pepper
½	cup boiling water		Paprika
1	cup frozen lima beans	½	red pepper as garnish
2	cups frozen whole-kernel corn		

Method

Sauté bacon until crisp. Remove from pan, drain and crumble. Remove bacon fat from pan. Add vegetable oil, heat and sauté onion and garlic until softened. Add boiling water and lima beans to skillet. Return water to boil. Cover and simmer 7 minutes. Add corn and simmer 5 minutes longer. Stir in cooked bacon, butter, parsley, salt, and pepper. Top with chopped pepper and a dash of paprika. Serve hot.

Basil Stewed Tomatoes
(Serves 4)

Ingredients

¼	cup olive oil	¼	teaspoon cayenne
1	onion, chopped		Salt to taste
1	stalk celery, chopped	¼	cup fresh basil leaves, chopped
6	large tomatoes, peeled, cut into eighths	¼	cup firmly packed fresh parsley leaves, chopped
3	cloves garlic, minced	¾	cup fresh breadcrumbs
2	teaspoons honey		

Method

Heat oil in a stainless steel or enamelled saucepan. Sauté onion and celery, stirring, for 8 minutes until the vegetables are softened. Add the tomatoes, garlic, honey, cayenne, and salt to taste, if desired. Bring the liquid to a simmer and simmer for 15 minutes, stirring occasionally. Add basil and parsley. Simmer for 5 minutes. Remove the pan from the heat. Let the stewed tomatoes stand, covered, for 5 minutes. Transfer the tomatoes to a heated serving dish.

Stuffed Tomatoes

Tomatoes and fresh basil are sufficient for a September lunch in our house; but when the garden overflows, we bake them together for dinner. (Serves 4)

Ingredients

4	large tomatoes, *or*	½	cup chopped zucchini
6	medium tomatoes	½	cup chopped mushrooms
1	onion	½	cup loosely packed basil leaves, chopped finely
2	tablespoons oil		
2	stalks celery	¼	cup grated Cheddar or Swiss cheese
1	green pepper		
1	cup fresh corn	¼	cup or more breadcrumbs

Method

Heat oven to 350°F (180°C). Cut tops off the tomatoes and carefully remove the pulp with a teaspoon, leaving the flesh around the sides. Salt the shells lightly and invert to drain. Chop the pulp.

Sauté the onion in oil. Add celery, green pepper, corn, zucchini, mushrooms, tomato pulp and basil. When the vegetables are hot, add 2 tablespoons of cheese and enough breadcrumbs to hold the mixture together. Salt to taste.

Fill the tomatoes while the filling is still hot. Place any extra filling in a greased baking dish just large enough to hold the tomatoes and put the tomatoes on top. Sprinkle with the remaining cheese and breadcrumbs.

Bake for 15 minutes.

Cracked Wheat, Watercress, and Pineapple Salad
(Serves 6)

Ingredients

2	cups bulgur (cracked wheat)		Pepper to taste
¾	cup olive oil	1	cup pineapple, cut in ½-inch cubes
4	cups chicken stock		
¼	cup lemon juice	1	cup firmly packed watercress leaves, coarsely chopped
1	large clove garlic, minced		
	Salt to taste		

Method

In a heavy skillet sauté the bulgur in ¼ cup of the olive oil over moderate heat, stirring, for 5 minutes. Add 4 cups of hot chicken stock. Bring the liquid to a boil and simmer the mixture, covered for 20 minutes, or until the liquid is absorbed. Set aside to cool.

In a large bowl combine ½ cup olive oil, the lemon juice, garlic, and salt and pepper to taste, if desired. Add the bulgur, pineapple and water-cress. Let the salad stand, covered for 2 hours. Transfer to a serving dish.

New Potato Salad

Here is a delicious salad dressing to lift the natural sweetness of new potatoes. Always dress potatoes when hot and serve them at room temperature. If refrigerated between mixing and serving, bring the salad out to room temperature, covered, for an hour or two. (Serves 8)

Ingredients

2½	pounds (1 kg) tiny, unpeeled new potatoes, washed	3	tablespoons olive oil
¼	cup wine vinegar	2	medium green onions, trimmed, rinsed and cut into 1-inch pieces
1	tablespoon Dijon mustard		
1	teaspoon salt	¼	cup chopped fresh dill
	Freshly ground black pepper	1	cup sour cream or yogurt

Method

In a 3-quart saucepan, cook the potatoes in boiling salted water over moderate heat just until tender, about 13 minutes.

Drain the potatoes in a colander and refresh them under cold running water. Cut them in half as soon as they can be handled and place in a large mixing bowl.

To make the dressing, whisk the wine vinegar, Dijon mustard, salt and freshly ground pepper together. Add the oil, continuing to whisk until it is incorporated.

Pour the dressing over the potatoes, add the green onions and dill. Toss gently. Salt and pepper to taste.

Fold in the sour cream or yogurt and let stand for 30 minutes before serving.

Avocado Dressing
(Makes 1 cup)

Ingredients

2	tablespoons vegetable oil	1	teaspoon fresh basil
1	large ripe avocado		Dash pepper
3	tablespoons lemon juice		Dash cayenne pepper
½	teaspoon salt		

Method

Mash avocado with fork. Shake all ingredients together in a jar or put everything in a blender and blend very briefly on low speed. Serve with lettuce and tomato salad.

Tarragon Vinaigrette
(Makes ¾ cup)

Ingredients

½	cup oil	1	teaspoon dried tarragon
1	tablespoon fresh lemon juice	1	teaspoon dried basil
5	tablespoons tarragon vinegar (see p. 121)	1	teaspoon celery seed
2	teaspoons sugar	2	teaspoons dried dill
1	teaspoon dried thyme		Freshly ground pepper to taste

Method

Whip together or, using the food processor with metal blade, process all ingredients until well mixed.

Herbed Buttermilk Dressing

Replacing some of the oil required in salad dressing recipes with buttermilk produces a light, thin dressing that adds tang to any salad. And there's a hidden bonus—fewer calories. (Makes about 1½ cups)

Ingredients

1	whole egg
1	large egg yolk
1	tablespoon white vinegar
2	teaspoons Dijon mustard
¾	teaspoon salt
1	small clove garlic, crushed
½	teaspoon dried thyme
½	teaspoon dried marjoram
½	teaspoon dried basil
½	teaspoon celery salt
½	cup vegetable oil (corn, safflower, sunflower, olive or other pure vegetable oil)
1	cup buttermilk
	White pepper

Method

Place all the ingredients except the oil, buttermilk and pepper into a food processor fitted with the steel blade. Process for 3 seconds. Then, with the motor running, add the vegetable oil and buttermilk in a thin stream. The longer you process, the thicker the dressing will become. Taste and add pepper as desired.

LOAVES, CAKES AND COOKIES

Gingerbread Muffins with Lemon Sauce

These are delicious, large and light. A lemon sauce would make them even more festive—especially when served warm on a cold day. (Makes 12 large muffins)

Ingredients

½	cup molasses	½	teaspoon cinnamon
⅔	cup boiling water	½	teaspoon nutmeg
2	cups all-purpose flour	½	teaspoon ginger
1	teaspoon baking soda	¾	cup brown sugar
1	teaspoon baking powder	½	cup oil
¼	teaspoon salt	1	egg, lightly beaten

Method

Preheat oven to 350°F (180°C). Blend the molasses and boiling water and let cool to room temperature. Measure flour, baking soda, baking powder, salt, spices, and brown sugar into a large bowl. Add oil, molasses-water mixture and egg and mix with dry ingredients until all dry ingredients are moistened. Do not overstir. The batter will be quite thin.

Pour into lightly oiled muffin tins, ⅔ full. Bake for 20–25 minutes. When baked, let stand for 5 minutes, then remove from tins. Serve warm.

Lemon Sauce
(Makes 1½ cups)

Ingredients

1	tablespoon cornstarch	2	tablespoons butter or
½	cup granulated sugar		margarine
¼	teaspoon salt	1	tablespoon grated lemon rind
¼	cup cold water	¼	cup lemon juice
1	cup boiling water		

Method

Combine the cornstarch, sugar, salt and cold water in a saucepan. Gradually stir in the boiling water. Cook over medium heat, stirring constantly, until thickened. Cover and cook 2 minutes longer, stirring occasionally. Remove from heat and blend in butter, lemon rind and lemon juice. Serve hot on gingerbread muffins.

Microwave Method

Combine all the ingredients in a 4-cup measure. Cook on full power for 3 minutes, stirring occasionally until thickened.

Ginger Jam Muffins

These are great for a holiday breakfast. (Makes 12)

Ingredients

1¼ cups all-purpose flour	1 egg
½ cup bran	½ cup milk
3 tablespoons brown sugar	6 tablespoons vegetable oil
3 teaspoons baking powder	½ cup ginger ale
⅛ teaspoon ground ginger	¼ cup raspberry or strawberry jam
⅓ cup chopped candied ginger	
½ cup flaked dried coconut	

Method

Preheat oven to 375°F (190°C). Generously grease a 12-cup muffin pan and sprinkle with granulated sugar.

Combine flour, bran, sugar, baking powder, ground ginger, candied ginger and coconut in large bowl. Beat egg, milk, vegetable oil, and ginger ale in smaller bowl. Quickly stir wet ingredients into dry ingredients, just until flour is moistened. Spoon one-half of the batter into muffin cups. Drop one teaspoon of jam in each cup and cover with remaining batter. Bake until muffins are lightly browned, about 25 minutes. Remove to cool.

Apple Graham Muffins

(Makes 12)

Ingredients

1 egg	1½ cups all-purpose flour
1¼ cups milk	3½ teaspoons baking powder
½ cup vegetable oil (corn, saf-flower, sunflower or other pure vegetable oil)	1 teaspoon cinnamon
	½ teaspoon salt
	Zest of ½ lemon
⅓ cup liquid honey	1 cup grated unpeeled apple (1 medium one)
1½ cups Graham wafer crumbs	

Method

Preheat oven to 400°F (200°C). Grease and sprinkle large muffin tins with sugar or line with paper baking cups. Beat the egg in a bowl with a fork. Blend in milk, oil and honey. Stir in crumbs.

Combine the flour, baking powder, cinnamon and salt in a large bowl. Stir the liquid mixture into the dry ingredients, just until moistened. Fold in lemon zest and grated apple. Spoon batter into muffin cups. Bake for about 20 minutes or until done. Cool and store in an airtight container.

Breakfast Prune Bread

A delightful quick bread, neither too sweet nor rich, perfect with the morning's first cup of tea or coffee. (Makes 2 loaves)

Ingredients

2⅔	cups flour	1	egg, beaten
4	tablespoons sugar	½	cup orange marmalade
1	tablespoon baking powder	⅓	cup vegetable oil (corn, saf-
1	teaspoon ground ginger		flower, sunflower or other
½	teaspoon salt		pure vegetable oil)
1½	cups pitted prunes	1⅓	cups chopped nuts
1¼	cups milk		Powdered sugar

Method

Combine flour, sugar, baking powder, ginger and salt. Set aside.

Coarsely chop the prunes, add to the milk and mix with the beaten egg, marmalade and oil. Stir in the dry ingredients, one-third at a time, and mix until just blended. Fold in the nuts.

Turn the batter into 2 greased and floured 8 inch × 4 inch × 3 inch (top inside measure) loaf pans. Bake at 350°F (180°C) for 1 hour, or until the bread tests done. Cool completely. Wrap in foil overnight. Dust the loaves with powdered sugar before slicing.

Food Processor Method

Measure the dry ingredients into the bowl of the food processor, fitted with the steel knife. Add the prunes and process on/off until they are chopped in pieces about the size of peas. Add nuts. Combine milk and oil together with the egg and marmalade and process quickly until the liquid ingredients are *just* incorporated. Proceed as above.

Zucchini Bread

Crunchy and rich in flavor, this is both a nutritious and delicious bread. We liked it slightly better without salt; you may too. (Makes 2 8 inch × 4 inch × 3 inch loaves)

Ingredients

2	tablespoons melted butter	¼	cup walnuts, chopped
¼	cup sugar	⅓	cup almonds, slivered
2¾	cups all-purpose flour	½	cup coconut, shredded
½	cup whole-wheat flour	⅓	cup golden raisins
2	teaspoons cinnamon		
1	teaspoon nutmeg	2½	cups shredded zucchini (2–3 medium zucchini, skins left on)
2	teaspoons baking soda		Zest of 1 lemon, grated
1	teaspoon baking powder		
1	teaspoon salt	4	eggs
		1½	cups sugar
		¾	cup vegetable oil

Method

Butter and sprinkle ¼ cup sugar into 2 loaf pans. Set aside. Preheat oven to 350°F (180°C).

Measure and blend together in a large bowl the flours, cinnamon, nutmeg, baking soda, baking powder, and salt. Add walnuts, almonds, coconut, raisins, shredded zucchini and lemon zest; toss to coat them all with dry ingredients.

Beat the eggs in a bowl until frothy, add sugar and oil, and beat until emulsified and creamy. Gradually stir liquid ingredients into flour and fruit mixture. Stir to combine well.

Divide batter equally and spread in prepared pans. Bake in preheated oven for 60 minutes, until cake tests done when a cake tester or toothpick inserted in the middle comes out dry.

Cool in pan for 10 minutes, then turn out onto racks to finish cooling. Wrap in foil.

This cake tastes better the next day. It may be iced with cream cheese frosting (see below), lemon glaze (see below) or another favorite of yours. It freezes well. If using icing with the cake, ice it, freeze it and then wrap in freezer paper or foil.

Lemon Glaze

½	cup sugar	4	tablespoons lemon juice

Mix sugar with the lemon juice and drizzle over cooled breads.

Cream Cheese Frosting
(Makes about 2½ cups)

Ingredients

1	8 ounce (250 g) package of cream cheese	1	tablespoon unsalted butter, softened
4	cups icing sugar	¼	teaspoon vanilla
1	teaspoon lemon juice		

Method

Blend cream cheese and sugar. Add lemon juice, butter and vanilla and mix well. Cool to room temperature. Spread on cooled breads.

Pineapple Bars
(Makes 16 bars)

Ingredients

1	cup all-purpose flour	½	cup butter, softened
½	teaspoon baking soda	1	14 ounce (328 mL) can crushed pineapple, drained (reserve juice)
¼	teaspoon salt		
½	cup brown sugar	3	tablespoons pineapple juice
1	cup quick-cooking rolled oats		

Frosting

½	cup sifted icing sugar	2-3	tablespoons pineapple juice

Method

Heat oven to 350°F (180°C). Combine the flour, soda, salt, brown sugar and oats. Blend butter into mixture with a pastry blender or fork until well mixed. Stir in crushed pineapple and juice. Spread into a lightly greased 8 inch square pan. Bake 20–25 minutes until golden brown. When cool, combine icing sugar and pineapple juice to make a spreading consistency. Glaze with icing.

Pumpkin Hermits

A great way to use up a Hallowe'en pumpkin, these cookies freeze well, either baked or unbaked. (Makes about 5 dozen)

Ingredients

¾	cup butter or margarine	1	teaspoon baking powder
1¼	cups brown sugar	1	teaspoon cinnamon
2	eggs	1	teaspoon nutmeg
1	teaspoon vanilla	½	teaspoon baking soda
1	cup cooked mashed pumpkin or squash	½	teaspoon cloves
		½	teaspoon salt
2	cups whole-wheat or all-purpose flour	1	cup finely chopped dates
		1	cup raisins
⅓	cup wheat germ (optional)	½	cup chopped walnuts

Method

Heat oven to 375°F (190°C). Lightly grease large baking sheet(s) or spread with parchment paper.

Cream the butter and sugar in a large bowl. Beat in the eggs and vanilla, then the pumpkin.

Add the flour, baking powder, baking soda, spices and salt, stirring well. Stir in dates, raisins and nuts.

Drop by spoonfuls onto prepared baking sheet. Bake 10–12 minutes or until cookies are light brown and top springs back when gently touched.

Queen of Nuts Cake

Carlo Middione always makes this cake a day before serving and stores it at room temperature. Frost just before serving with chocolate butter cream or just sprinkle with confectioner's sugar, if you prefer. (Serves 10 or more)

Ingredients

1	tablespoon soft, unsalted butter	6	ounces semi-sweet chocolate, grated
3	tablespoons fine breadcrumbs	1	teaspoon pure vanilla extract (or flavoring)
1	cup almonds, pecans, or walnuts (or mixture of all three)		Freshly grated rind of 1 large orange
⅔	cup granulated sugar (extra fine if possible)	5	large eggs, separated

Method

Butter a 9-inch cake pan and sprinkle with breadcrumbs to cover evenly all over. Set aside. Preheat oven to 350°F (180°C).

Grind the nuts very finely (pulverize if possible), using a blender, food processor or hand grinder, passing two or three times. Mix the nuts and sugar in a bowl. Add the grated chocolate with the vanilla, grated orange peel and the egg yolks. Mix again. The mixture will be quite dense and hard to turn. Beat the egg whites until smooth and shiny (at room temperature, in order to get the best texture and volume) in an unlined copper bowl with a whisk or with an electric mixer. Be careful not to overbeat. Add a few spoonfuls of the beaten egg whites to the mixture to loosen it. Then, gently but thoroughly, fold the entire mixture into the remaining beaten egg whites. Pour into the prepared cake pan (see note) and bake for about 35–40 minutes. The cake is done when the top is nicely firm to the touch. Remove the cake from the oven and set on a cooling rack for 10–15 minutes. Turn the cake out of the pan.

The bottom may be stuck a little; this is normal. Finish cooling the turned-out cake on the rack. You can store this cake for several days well covered at room temperature. Storing it in the refrigerator will make it somewhat gummy. Either way it is stored, the cake tastes better the day after it is baked, and still better the day after that! When ready to serve, sprinkle the cake generously with powdered sugar, or decorate with dark chocolate butter cream (following).

Note. Do not overfill the cake pan. The mixture should come about two-thirds of the way up. If you overfill the pan, the cake may collapse upon cooling. If it does, don't worry. Serve it anyway. The flavor will not be affected, although the texture will be more like a delicious nutty fudge. Nuts too coarsely chopped will also cause the cake to collapse slightly. Again, don't worry....

Chocolate Butter Cream
(Makes about 1½ cups)

Ingredients

1	cup sweet butter	4	tablespoons dark cocoa, sifted
1¼	cups powdered sugar, sifted		(use lighter cocoa if preferred)
2	egg yolks		

Method

Place butter into a mixing bowl and whip until light and airy and very white in color. Then, while still whipping, add the sugar a little at a time until all of it has been incorporated. Add the egg yolks and continue to whip until they are well blended. Add the cocoa a tablespoon at a time and continue to whip until all is blended and mixture is a nice even color. The color will be lighter at this stage than it will be later on.

If you find that the mixture is quite dense and difficult to handle *add 1 tablespoon* of very hot water—just under the boiling point. Whip rapidly. This should immediately loosen up the cream and also make it even glossier. You can do this up to three times with no problem.

Spread the edges of the cake with some cream and then decorate the top as you like with piping or rosettes. The cream will keep very well in the refrigerator for a couple of weeks. You can freeze it indefinitely in a plastic container. In either case, when you want to use it let it come to room temperature slowly (take it out the night before you want to use it) and gently re-whip it. You can make a half-recipe but it is better and easier to work with larger amounts. If you don't need this much at one time, freeze the rest until needed.

Buttermilk Chocolate Cake

Campton Place Hotel at Union Square in San Francisco is a small, luxury hotel boasting one of North America's finest dining rooms. When I wrote and asked the chef for the two cake recipes I'd sampled on a recent visit, he swiftly obliged. The chocolate cake is moist, light and delicious; the Ginger Spice Cake (see p. 100) is all that and more. They're simple to make, too. (Serves 6–8)

Ingredients

5	ounces unsweetened chocolate	1½	cups granulated sugar
⅔	cup sweet butter	1¾	cups cake and pastry flour
¾	cup buttermilk	½	teaspoon baking soda
5	large egg yolks	5	large egg whites

Method

Measure cake pans. This amount is fine for 2 9-inch cake pans or 2 $8\frac{3}{8}$ inch × $1\frac{5}{8}$ inch (21.3 × 4.1 cm) foil pans. Preheat oven to 350°F (180°C).

Butter the sides and bottoms of two cake pans (or two foil pans as above). Then line the bottom of each pan with parchment paper. Proceed to butter the paper and finish by lightly flouring each pan.

Place the chocolate and butter in the top of a double boiler and melt over boiling water. When melted, add the buttermilk slowly, stirring constantly. Set aside and let cool.

Combine the yolks and sugar in a mixing bowl and beat until smooth. Then add the chocolate mixture slowly to the yolk mixture. Set aside.

Sift the flour and baking soda. Beat the egg whites in a mixing bowl until stiff but not dry. Fold the beaten egg whites into the chocolate mixture; then fold in the flour mixture. When sufficiently mixed, pour batter into the two cake pans. Bake for about 30 minutes or until a tester comes out clean. Turn out onto two cake racks, remove paper and allow to cool.

Chocolate Glaze

Ingredients

3 ounces semi-sweet chocolate	1 8 ounce (250 mL) container 35% cream
$1\frac{1}{2}$ ounces unsweetened chocolate	$\frac{1}{4}$ cup granulated sugar

Method

Melt the chocolate in a double boiler and remove from heat. In a saucepan, bring $\frac{1}{2}$ cup cream to a boil and add to the melted chocolate. Remove from heat and let cool. In a chilled bowl or food processor, whip the balance of the cream with the sugar. Add to chocolate mixture. Spread between layers of the cake and over top and sides of cake. Decorate with finely chopped pecans or sifted icing sugar.

Ginger Spice Cake
(Serves 10)

Ingredients

2¾ cups cake and pastry flour
1 tablespoon ground ginger
½ teaspoon ground cinnamon
½ teaspoon ground nutmeg
½ teaspoon ground cloves
1 teaspoon salt
1 teaspoon baking soda

½ cup unsalted butter
1 cup molasses
½ cup dark brown sugar
1 cup buttermilk
¼ cup freshly squeezed orange juice
2 eggs, slightly beaten

Method

Preheat oven to 350°F (180°C). Butter and flour one 9-inch round cake pan. (See Chocolate Buttermilk Cake for alternative pan sizes.)

Sift cake and pastry flour once, then sift together the dry ingredients and set aside in a bowl. In a small saucepan, melt butter, then add molasses and brown sugar. Set aside to cool.

When the butter mixture is cool, stir into dry ingredients and mix thoroughly. Add buttermilk, orange juice and eggs.

Pour into cake pan and bake for 35–40 minutes until done. Turn out on cake rack to cool. Serve with Orange Curd Sauce (see below).

Orange Curd Sauce
(Makes 1 cup sauce)

Ingredients

Zest and juice of 2 oranges
1 cup sugar
4 tablespoons unsalted butter

2 egg yolks
2 whole eggs

Method

Combine all ingredients in a saucepan and cook until thickened, whisking while it cooks. Strain, cool and serve with Ginger Spice Cake.

DESSERTS

Sabayon with Fresh Fruit
(Serves 4)

Ingredients

3	egg yolks		¼	cup Marsala wine
1	whole egg		¼	cup dry white wine
3	tablespoons sugar		½	teaspoon lemon juice

Method

Mix all ingredients with a beater or wire whisk in the top of a double boiler. Place over boiling water and cook gently, beating constantly, until just thickened. This takes about 5 minutes.

Serve warm over fresh fruit such as strawberries, kiwi or pineapple.

Crème Anglaise

Crème anglaise is just a fancy name for basic custard, and is sometimes called a boiled or poured custard. It can be used hot or cold, served with poached fruit such as rhubarb, apples or summer berries. (Makes 1½ cups)

Ingredients

4	egg yolks		1–1½	cups milk
½	cup sugar		1	teaspoon vanilla extract
	Pinch of salt			

Method

Beat egg yolks slightly with a wire whisk. Gradually add sugar mixed with a pinch of salt and continue beating until well blended. Scald milk in a heavy saucepan at medium-low heat until small bubbles appear around edges of the pan. In a steady stream, pour the milk over yolk mixture and continue to beat. Return mixture to saucepan. Heat over low heat stirring constantly with a wooden spoon. The mixture will become thick and smooth. Add flavoring. Serve warm or chilled.

Note: Stir the custard as it cools to prevent separation. For a thicker sauce use 1 cup milk.

Blueberry Lemon Mousse
(Serves 4)

Ingredients

2	eggs, separated	2	tablespoons water
¼	cup granulated sugar	⅛	teaspoon cream of tartar
1	teaspoon lemon zest	1	cup fresh or thawed frozen blueberries
2	tablespoons lemon juice		

Method

Beat together egg yolks, sugar, lemon zest, lemon juice and water in a small saucepan. Cook over low heat, stirring constantly until the mixture thickens and coats a metal spoon, 5–7 minutes. Cool quickly by setting the pan in a bowl of ice water and stirring for a few minutes. Cover and refrigerate to chill thoroughly, about 20 minutes.

In a small bowl, beat egg whites and cream of tartar until stiff but not dry. To test, tilt the bowl. If the whites do not slip out, they are ready. Gently fold the cooled custard sauce and blueberries into the beaten egg whites. Spoon into 4 dessert dishes and serve immediately. This dessert may be made up to 3 hours ahead and kept refrigerated until serving time.

Frozen Grapes

Ingredients

Seedless grapes

Method

Cut grapes into small clusters and freeze. Serve with a mint leaf garnish.

Grapefruit, Apple and Berry Salad
(Serves 2)

Ingredients

1	grapefruit	2	tablespoons sugar
1	apple, peeled	1/4	cup fresh or frozen blueberries or raspberries
2	teaspoons kirsch		

Method

Peel grapefruit and hold over a bowl to collect juice while sectioning it. Squeeze to remove juice after sectioning. Slice the apple into grapefruit and add grapefruit juice. Taste and add sugar and kirsch. Toss and combine with berries. Serve cold.

Peach Parisian
(Serves 2)

Ingredients

2	large, fresh peaches, peeled *or*	1/2	cup sour cream or yogurt
4	halves canned peaches, drained	1	tablespoon cocoa
1/2	cup vanilla ice cream *or*		

Method

Cut the fresh peaches into halves and sweeten with sugar or sweetener, if desired. Arrange the peach halves in a small serving dish. Fill the centre with ice cream, sour cream or yogurt and sprinkle with cocoa. Serve cold.

Quick Rum and Raisin Ice Cream
(Serves 2)

Ingredients

3	tablespoons dark rum	1/2	cup sugar
1/4	cup raisins	1/4	cup water
1	tablespoon butter		Vanilla ice cream

Method

Soak the raisins in the rum for ½–1 hour. Combine all the ingredients except ice cream and cook over low heat, stirring constantly until sugar is dissolved and the sauce is hot. Serve over vanilla ice cream.

Lo-Cal Cheesecake
(Serves 8–10)

Ingredients

Crust

⅔	cup crushed Graham wafers	¼	teaspoon cinnamon
3	tablespoons finely chopped pecans	1	tablespoon skim milk powder
1	tablespoon wheat germ	3	tablespoons unsalted butter, melted

Combine ingredients and press into an 8-inch spring form pan. Set aside for filling.

Filling

2	egg whites	1	tablespoon corn starch
1	whole egg	¾	cup sugar
1	pound (500 g) 2% cottage cheese, drained and measured (approximately 3 cups)	1	teaspoon vanilla extract
		1	teaspoon lemon extract
		½	cup yogurt

Method

Preheat oven to 375°F (190°C). Combine all the ingredients, except yogurt, in large blender jar or food processor. Blend for 1 minute or until ingredients are mixed smoothly. Pour into crust and bake for 10 minutes. Lower oven temperature to 225°F (105°C) and continue baking for 45 minutes. Open oven and spread yogurt over the cake. Continue baking for a further 15 minutes. Turn off oven and leave cake until oven is cool. Refrigerate.

Cranberry Cheesecake
(Serves 10–12)

Ingredients

Nut Crust

2 tablespoons icing sugar
½ teaspoon cinnamon
1 cup ground walnuts

¾ cup chopped walnuts
3 tablespoons unsalted butter, melted

Filling

2 pounds (1 kg) cream cheese, softened, or 1 pound cottage and 1 pound cream cheese

½ cup sugar
6 eggs
1 tablespoon lemon juice

Cranberry Topping

⅓ cup water
⅔ cup sugar

2½ cups fresh cranberries
½ teaspoon cinnamon

Method

Crust

Preheat oven to 400°F (200°C). In a bowl, sift together icing sugar and cinnamon. Add ground walnuts and stir. Stir in chopped walnuts and melted butter. Combine well and press evenly into the bottom of a 9-inch springform pan. Place the pan on a cookie sheet to catch any melted butter. Bake crust until it is dry and edges are slightly brown, 5–8 minutes. Remove from oven and put on a wire rack to cool. Lower oven temperature to 350°F (180°C).

Filling

Beat softened cream cheese in a large mixing bowl until it is light. Gradually beat in sugar and then add the eggs, one at a time. Stir in lemon juice. Pour into cooled crust.

Bake cheesecake at 350°F (180°C) until a toothpick inserted into the centre comes out almost clean, about 45 minutes. Turn oven off and leave the cake in until it has cooled, about 2 hours. Loosen sides of cake from pan.

Topping

In a saucepan, stir together water and sugar over medium heat. Bring syrup to boil and let it boil for one minute. Stir in the cranberries. Cover pan and lower heat. Let the sauce cook until most of the berries have popped and the consistency is quite thick, about 3 minutes. Stir in cinnamon and remove from heat. Force sauce through a sieve or food mill and set aside.

Pour the cranberry topping over the top of the cake and chill overnight or at least for several hours in refrigerator. Remove rim of springform just before cutting.

Sweet Potato Pecan Pie
(Makes 1 9-inch pie)

Ingredients

	Pastry for single 9-inch crust pie	½	beaten egg
		2	tablespoons sugar
1	cup cooked, mashed sweet potatoes	1	tablespoon heavy cream
		½	cup chopped pecans
1	tablespoon butter	¾	cup sugar
¼	cup firmly packed light brown sugar	2½	eggs
		¾	cup dark corn syrup
1	tablespoon vanilla	1½	tablespoons melted butter
¼	teaspoon cinnamon		Pinch salt
⅛	teaspoon nutmeg		Pinch cinnamon
⅛	teaspoon allspice	2	teaspoons vanilla
¼	teaspoon salt		

Method

Roll dough to fit a deep 9-inch pie plate. Press the pastry into plate and flute edges.

Combine sweet potatoes, butter, brown sugar, vanilla, spices, beaten ½ egg, sugar and cream; beat at medium speed until mixture is smooth. Spread on bottom of pastry shell; sprinkle with pecans.

Combine ¾ cup sugar, 2½ eggs, corn syrup, melted butter, salt, cinnamon and vanilla and beat well. Pour over pecans.

Bake at 400°F (200°C) for 10 minutes. Lower temperature to 325°F (160°C) and continue baking for 35–40 minutes or until a knife inserted into the middle of the filling comes out clean. Cool. Top each slice with a dollop of whipped cream.

Apple Strudel Filling

(Makes 2 12–18 inch strudels)

Ingredients

5	pounds (2.3 kg) cooking apples, each cut into 12 slices	1	cup raisins
1½	cups brown sugar		Pinch salt
2	cups toasted coarsely ground walnuts		Lemon juice
		1	teaspoon cinnamon
3	cups cake, cookie, or Graham cracker crumbs	1½	cups clarified butter (p. 33)
4	tablespoons butter	1	recipe strudel pastry (pp. 74–78)

Method

Mix together thoroughly apples, brown sugar, walnuts, raisins, salt, lemon juice and cinnamon. The filling should be thick, strongly flavored and moist. Add more lemon juice and cinnamon to suit your taste, if desired. Divide in half. Sauté the crumbs in the 4 tablespoons of butter and cool.

Preheat oven to 375°F (190°C). Paint the whole strudel sheet lightly with clarified butter. Scatter half the crumbs in the centre and fold the two outside edges in so they just meet in the centre. The dough will be 18 inches wide. Lightly butter the surface and sprinkle with remaining crumbs. Arrange one half of the apple filling in a long pile across the base of the dough—leave a couple of inches at either end. Fold the flap of dough over the filling and roll the strudel, buttering after each half turn. Check for flour and brush away. When the strudel is rolled up, transfer to a baking sheet and tuck under the ends. At this stage, it may be frozen for later baking. If so, bake immediately from the freezer. Repeat this process with the second half of dough and other half of filling.

Poke strudel top with a skewer in 4 places as air vents. Bake at 375°F (190°C) for 10 minutes, then 350°F (180°C) for 30–35 minutes. Brush 3 or 4 times during baking with fresh clarified butter (not that in pan). Strudel may crack in the centre toward the end of baking, but this is normal. Brush with butter as soon as it comes from oven. Cool on the baking sheet and slice. Serve warm with unsweetened whipped cream.

Fruit Strudel Filling

(Makes 2 12–18 inch strudels)

Ingredients

4	cups dried fruit — pears, apricots, apples, prunes	2	teaspoons cinnamon
1½	cups dried figs, chopped	2	teaspoons grated lemon rind
2	cups red wine	¼	cup kirsch
2	cups water (more or less, depending on fruit)	1	cup sugar
		1½	cups chopped walnuts

Assembling

3	cups cake, cookie or Graham cracker crumbs	1½	cups clarified butter (p. 33)
		1	recipe strudel pastry (pp. 74–78)

Method

Combine dried fruit and figs in wine and enough water to barely cover. Add the cinnamon and lemon and simmer until just tender. Add kirsch and sugar to taste. Let stand for at least an hour until all the liquid is absorbed (overnight is best). Stir in the nuts. Taste and adjust. The filling must be very flavorful. Divide filling in half.

Preheat oven to 375°F (190°C). Paint the whole strudel sheet lightly with clarified butter. Scatter half the crumbs in the centre and fold the two outside edges in so they just meet in the centre. The dough will be 18 inches wide. Lightly butter the surface and sprinkle with remaining crumbs. Arrange one half of the apple filling in a long pile across the base of the dough—leave a couple of inches at either end. Fold the flap of dough over the filling and roll the strudel, buttering after each half turn. Check for flour and brush away. When the strudel is rolled up, transfer to a baking sheet and tuck under the ends. At this stage, it may be frozen for later baking. If so, bake immediately from the freezer. Repeat this process with the second half of dough and other half of filling.

Poke strudel top with a skewer in 4 places as air vents. Bake at 375°F (190°C) for 10 minutes, then at 350°F (180°C) for 30 35 minutes. Brush 3 or 4 times during the baking with fresh clarified butter (not that in pan). Strudel may crack in the centre toward the end of baking, but this is normal. Brush with butter as soon as it comes from oven. Cool on the baking sheet. Slice and serve warm, sprinkled with sieved icing sugar and/or unsweetened whipped cream. May be reheated for crisper pastry.

Apple Raisin Pie

Ingredients

1½ cups raisins
1 cup water
½ cup sugar
1 tablespoon flour
½ teaspoon cinnamon
1 tablespoon lemon juice

4 cups pared and diced apples (4–6 apples)
½ cup grated old Cheddar cheese

Pastry for 2 crust 9-inch pie
1 lightly beaten egg yolk
Sugar

Method

Preheat oven to 425°F (220°C). Boil raisins and water in a large saucepan until the liquid is almost absorbed, about 5–7 minutes. Meanwhile, in a small bowl, mix sugar, flour and cinnamon. Stir into the raisin mixture with lemon juice and apples. Turn into a pastry-lined pie pan; sprinkle with cheese. Cover with the top crust, cutting slits for steam to escape. Brush with egg yolk and sprinkle with sugar. Bake for 10 minutes; reduce heat to 350°F (180°C) and bake 45–55 minutes longer or until the pastry is golden brown. Serve warm or cold.

Lemon Chiffon Cake with Lemon Filling

Ingredients

2 cups cake and pastry flour, sifted

1½ cups sugar
3 teaspoons baking powder
1 teaspoon salt
½ cup vegetable oil

7 egg yolks, unbeaten

¾ cup cold water
1 teaspoon vanilla
2 teaspoons grated lemon rind
7 egg whites
½ teaspoon cream of tartar
1 cup finely chopped pecans (optional)

Method

Preheat oven to 325°F (160°C). Sift the flour and measure. Resift the flour with sugar, baking powder and salt in a large bowl. Make a well in the middle. Add, in order, oil, egg yolks, water, vanilla and lemon rind. Beat with a spoon until smooth.

Beat egg whites for 30 seconds. Add cream of tartar and continue beating until whites form *very stiff peaks*. Do not underbeat. Gradually pour the egg yolk mixture over the whites, gently folding with a rubber scraper until just blended. Pour into an ungreased 10-inch round tube pan. Bake for 55 minutes; then raise temperature to 350°F (180°C) for 10–15 minutes.

Invert the cake pan on a funnel or glass until the cake is quite cool. Remove and place on cake plate. If leaving unfilled, decorate with a sprinkle of icing sugar.

Lemon Filling

Ingredients

¾	cup sugar	1	grated rind of lemon
¼	cup cornstarch	3	egg yolks
1	cup water	1	tablespoon butter
¼	cup lemon juice		

Method

Place all the ingredients together in a blender or processor, cover and process for 20 seconds. Pour into a saucepan and cook over low heat, stirring constantly until mixture has thickened and is smooth. Cool before using to fill cake.

Place the cake upside down on waxed paper. Slice the top from the cake. Now make a tunnel. Cut the centre out of the cake by slicing parallel to the outside, bottom and middle edges all the way around. Be careful not to cut through to the bottom. There should be 1 inch of cake remaining on bottom and sides.

Completely fill the cake with cooled filling, pushing the filling down to fill any holes that might appear when the cake is sliced.

Replace the top of the cake and press gently. Set the cake on a large plate or cake tray. Frost the cake with sweetened whipped cream that has been flavored with lemon extract, or a favorite liqueur such as crème de menthe.

Dione Lucas's Soufflé Chocolate Roll

As the pièce de résistance to that special dinner party, this dessert recipe has to rate among the top. Because the chocolate roll contains no flour, its texture, although cakelike, has an airy lightness few ordinary cakes can approach. (Serves 8–10)

Ingredients

2	tablespoons melted butter	6	egg whites
6	ounces semi-sweet chocolate, coarsely chopped	¼	teaspoon salt
2	tablespoons strong coffee	⅓	cup unsweetened cocoa (for dusting)
6	egg yolks		
½	cup sugar		
		1½	cups heavy cream, chilled
		2	teaspoons Cognac or brandy

Method

Cut a piece of waxed or parchment paper 20 inches × 11 inches so that when laid in a jellyroll pan measuring 16 inches × 11 inches × ½ inch, the paper will be 2 inches longer at each end than the pan. Lightly brush the pan with melted butter, lay the paper on top and brush the paper with melted butter. The longer ends act as handles with which to remove the cake. Set aside.

Preheat the oven to 350°F (180°C) and place oven rack in the centre.

Place the chocolate pieces and the coffee in the top of a double boiler and set over simmering water. Make certain that the top does not touch the water. Heat until the chocolate is melted and smooth, stirring well. Remove pan to the counter and allow the chocolate mixture to cool.

Meanwhile, in a medium-sized bowl, beat the yolks until they are light and creamy. Gradually add the sugar, beating until the mixture is thick and golden yellow. Slowly beat in the melted chocolate, and continue to beat until the mixture is smooth and glossy.

In a large bowl, add the salt to the egg whites and beat until they hold firm, glossy peaks and do not slide when the bowl is turned upside down.

Beat about one-quarter of the whites vigorously into the soufflé base. Then, using a rubber spatula, pour the soufflé base over the remaining egg whites and gently combine them, using the spatula to cut and fold and bring the heavier chocolate mixture up and over the lighter whites as you rotate the bowl. Fold gently just until no streaks of white show, being careful not to overfold so you don't lose the air you have incorporated into the whites.

Pour the batter into the prepared pan, spreading it evenly with a rubber spatula. Place the pan in the preheated oven and bake for about

15–18 minutes, or until a toothpick or cake tester comes out clean and dry.

As soon as the cake is done, lift the pan from the oven and set it on a cake rack. Wet a clean dish towel in cold water, wring it out, and completely cover the top of the cake with it. Then cover the wet towel with a dry towel and let the cake cool to room temperature.

When the cake is cool, gently lift off the dry and then the wet towels—a little of the cake will come away—and run a small knife down the edge of the pan to loosen the sides. Through a fine sieve, sift the cocoa evenly over the top of the cake.

Cut a piece of heavy-duty aluminum foil about 2 inches larger than the pan on all sides and place it over the top of the cake. Then, holding the pan and foil tightly with both hands, invert the pan so that the cake falls onto the foil, cocoa-covered side down and the bottom of the jellyroll pan facing up.

Place the foil on your work surface, remove the baking pan, and carefully strip off the wax paper liner (which will now be on top). Then, with a sharp knife, cut away any crusty edges.

Pour the heavy cream into a chilled, medium-sized bowl and beat with a rotary or electric beater until the cream holds a shape. Add the Cognac or brandy, and continue beating until the cream is stiff enough to hold soft peaks. Do not overbeat.

With a rubber spatula, gently spread the whipped cream over the entire surface of the cake.

With the long side of the cake parallel to you, use the foil to help roll the cake over on itself. Continue lifting the foil higher and higher with both hands until you have a complete roll with the seam on the bottom. The cake will probably crack during the rolling, but don't be concerned. You can sift additional cocoa over the top of the roll to camouflage any bad cracks.

With scissors or a knife, cut away all the exposed foil along the long sides of the roll, but leave the foil under the roll and at either short end. Using these protruding foil ends as handles, carefully transfer the roll, cradlelike, to a large serving platter or jelly-roll board. Cut off all exposed foil and, if you like, finish the roll by piping rosettes of whipped cream around the sides.

Try to fill and roll the dessert no more than an hour before serving so you won't have to refrigerate it, which will stiffen the chocolate and cause the roll to lose its airy texture. If necessary, the roll can be refrigerated for a few hours but not longer, since the cream will break and the roll will become soggy.

Adapted from *The Michael Field Egg Cookbook*, published by Holt, Rinehart and Winston.

Christmas Candied Fruit Tart

If you sometimes feel jaded and begin to wonder if anyone notices all the effort you put into cooking special delights and family favorites for the Christmas holiday, try this recipe. If you were in danger of being taken for granted before, you won't be after serving this!

Ingredients

Pastry

1½	cups cake and pastry flour		2	egg yolks
½	cup butter		2	teaspoons vanilla extract
3	tablespoons sugar			Water to form a smooth dough
1	cup hazelnuts or filberts, coarsely chopped			(between 3–4 tablespoons)

Method

Preheat oven to 400°F (200°C). Combine, either by hand or with the dough hook of an electric mixer, the flour, butter and sugar. Then add hazelnuts, egg yolks, vanilla and enough water to form a smooth dough.

Press down and around the edges of a greased and floured 10-inch springform pan. Bake the shell in the preheated oven for 20 minutes, until crisp, like shortbread. Cool. Lower oven temperature to 375°F (190°C).

Ingredients

Filling

¾	cup golden raisins		½	cup Graham cracker crumbs
¼	cup dark rum		⅓	cup glacéed orange rind, chopped
¼	cup hot water			
⅓	cup whole blanched almonds		⅓	cup glacéed citron, chopped
1	teaspoon vanilla		¼	cup sugar
½	teaspoon cinnamon		2	egg yolks
¼	teaspoon ground cloves			
½	cup walnut pieces		4	egg whites
			½	cup sugar

Method

Soak the raisins in the dark rum and hot water until plump. In a food processor fitted with the steel blade process the almonds for 10 seconds, add the raisins including the liquid, the vanilla, cinnamon, cloves, walnuts, Graham cracker crumbs, orange rind, citron, sugar and egg yolks and process the mixture for 10 seconds. Spread the filling evenly in the cooled, baked shell.

Bake the tart in the middle rack of the preheated 375°F (190°C) oven for 20 minutes. Remove from oven.

Whip egg whites until frothy and gradually add the sugar to make a stiff, glossy meringue. Cover the tart with meringue and bake at 375°F (190°C) for another 10 minutes.

Let cool, remove sides of springform pan and place on a serving dish. Use a hot knife, dipped in water to cut tart.

Christmas Fruit Torte

Ingredients

1½ cups cake and pastry flour	1½ cups citron, cut into small strips
½ cup butter	
1 cup sugar	1 cup candied pineapple, cut into small pieces
3 egg yolks, well-beaten	
1 teaspoon almond extract	3 egg whites, beaten stiff
½ cup milk	1 8 ounce (250 mL) container 35% cream, whipped
1 cup grated coconut	
1½ cups almonds, blanched and slivered	3 tablespoons sugar

Method

Sift flour and measure. Set aside. Butter and flour 3 8-inch cake pans. Set aside. Preheat oven to 350°F (180°C). Measure and chop fruits and nuts.

In a large bowl, cream butter and add sugar slowly. When thoroughly creamed together, beat in egg yolks and almond extract. Add the sifted flour and milk alternately until well mixed.

Stir into the batter the coconut, almonds, citron, and pineapple. Carefully fold in egg whites. Pour batter into prepared pans. Bake for 30–40 minutes, or until cake tests done. Turn out onto cake racks to cool.

Whip the cream and add sugar. Arrange one layer on a serving plate. Spread with ⅓ sweetened whipped cream. Cover with next layer, spread with cream and top with final layer. Spread cream over top and garnish with cherries and grated coconut, if desired.

Buttermilk Custard Pie

Buttermilk left over? There is no better way to use it than in this creamy custard pie. Less expensive and lower in calories than many other kinds of custard pie, we're sure you'll agree that the results are delicious. (Serves 4-6)

Ingredients

1	unbaked pastry or oatmeal crumb pie shell	3	tablespoons flour
		1	teaspoon vanilla
3	slightly beaten eggs	1	teaspoon cinnamon
1	cup sugar	1	tablespoon lemon juice
¼	cup melted butter	¾	cup buttermilk

Method

Whisk together the eggs, sugar, butter, flour, vanilla and cinnamon. Stir in lemon juice and buttermilk. Pour into unbaked pie shell. Bake in preheated oven at 425°F (220°C) for 10 minutes, then reduce heat to 350°F (180°C) and bake another 20–25 minutes, until set. Cool on a rack and chill. Garnish with fresh berries or sliced peaches.

Sweet Carrot Pudding

A traditional, sweet carrot dessert is a lovely finalé to a curry dinner. (Serves 4-6)

Ingredients

¼	cup coarsely chopped blanched almonds	½	teaspoon ground cardamom
		2	tablespoons heavy cream
6	finely grated carrots	1	teaspoon grated lemon rind
4	tablespoons sugar		Lemon juice
3	cups milk		Grated almonds

Method

Mix together the almonds, carrots, sugar, milk and cardamom. Simmer covered, very slowly, on low heat until carrots absorb all of the milk, about 2 hours. Stir every 15 minutes. Cool, then add cream and lemon rind. Serve sprinkled with lemon juice and topped with grated almonds.

ET CETERA

No-Salt Seasoning Powder
(Makes about 2 tablespoons*)

Ingredients

Grated peel of ½ lemon
2 teaspoons chopped parsley
½ teaspoon garlic powder
½ teaspoon oregano or basil, crushed

½ teaspoon marjoram, crushed
¼ teaspoon allspice
¼ teaspoon black pepper

Method

Combine all ingredients and store in the refrigerator in a covered jar. To use, sprinkle as desired over meat, poultry or fish before broiling or baking.

Low Calorie Crème Fraîche

Use this sweet-sour sauce to lift the flavors of pan-sautéed chicken, meat, fish and vegetables. Add herbs and leave the salt in the cupboard! Contains 236 calories per cup. (Makes about 1½ cups)

Ingredients

½ cup low-fat plain yogurt
½ cup sour cream

½ cup evaporated skim milk

Method

Gently stir all ingredients in bowl until evenly blended. Store in an airtight jar in refrigerator. Stir before using.

---

*Contains about 1mg sodium and 2 calories per teaspoon.

Crunchy Pie Crust

A rich crunchy crust for holiday pies. (Makes 1 9-inch pie crust)

Ingredients

1	cup quick rolled oats, uncooked	⅓	cup brown sugar
⅓	cup sifted flour	½	teaspoon salt
		⅓	cup melted shortening or butter

Method

Mix together the oats, flour, sugar and salt. Add shortening and mix until crumbly. Press firmly into the bottom and on the sides of a 9-inch pie plate. Place a smaller pie plate on top to hold the crumbs in place. Bake at 375°F (190°C) until crust is brown, about 15 minutes. Remove the small pie plate 2 minutes after the crust comes from the oven. Cool and fill with your favorite pie filling.

Roasted Pumpkin or Squash Seeds

Roasted seeds may be served alone or mixed with salted nuts or sunflower seeds. (Makes 1 cup)

Ingredients

1	cup unwashed pumpkin or squash seeds	½	teaspoon salt
2	teaspoons vegetable oil	½	teaspoon Worcestershire sauce
		¼	teaspoon celery salt (optional)

Method

Toss ingredients in a small bowl to mix well. Spread the mixture on a baking sheet and bake at 250°F (120°C) for 1 hour or until seeds are brown and crunchy. Shake occasionally during baking.

Lime Marmalade
(Makes about 3 jelly jars)

Ingredients

6	small limes	¾	cup sugar per cup of fruit and
3	lemons		juice (measured after first
	Water		boiling)

Method

Scrub the fruit well and remove the thin skin layer with a zester or vegetable peeler so that it is in thin strips. Cut the fruit into small pieces, remove and discard the pits. Measure the fruit and juice. Measure 3 times as much water as the amount of fruit and juice and add. Soak overnight.

Simmer the mixture for 20 minutes, add sugar and let stand again for about 12 hours. Use a deep, flat-bottomed stainless steel or enamelled pot with a cover.

After standing time, cook with the lid off. Stir constantly with a metal spoon. Remove any foam that rises to the top until the liquid becomes clear and shiny (approximately 20–40 minutes). Test if marmalade is done.

To test if done
Always remove pan from heat when testing. Drop a spoonful of the hot liquid onto a thoroughly chilled plate (leave it in the freezer for 5-10 minutes). Place in the refrigerator for 5 minutes. If jellied by this time, the marmalade is ready; if not, continue cooking a few minutes longer, and again test for doneness. When ready, pour into sterilized hot jelly glasses.

To prepare jars
Before preparing fruit, check you jar supply. You do not need canning jars, but the jars must be uncracked and free of nicks. I prefer clear glass jars—they look pretty. Before boiling up the fruit mixture, wash, rinse and set jars on a heatproof tray. A jellyroll pan (sturdy baking sheet with sides) is most useful for this job. Include with the jars a funnel and a small heatproof pitcher for pouring the hot marmalade into the jars. Heat jars at 250°F (120°C) for 15 minutes or leave in oven until needed.

To fill jars
With the funnel, fill jars to within ½ inch of the top. Let cool 30 minutes. Melt paraffin wax in a metal tea pot, set in a saucepan of simmering water and pour a thin layer over the marmalade. Tilt the jar to extend wax up to rim. Let jars cool completely and add a second layer of wax. Cover with clean lids, wipe if necessary and label. Store away from heat, light and dampness.

Tarragon Vinegar

The advantage to making your own vinegar is that you can make the flavoring as piquant or mild as you want. Fresh tarragon is best for making this vinegar but dried can be used—2 tablespoons of dried tarragon to 2½ cups vinegar. If you want to add a decorative touch, a spray of tarragon can be placed in the bottle once the vinegar has been strained. (Makes 2½ cups)

Ingredients

2½ cups white wine vinegar
2   ounces fresh tarragon, stalks and leaves bruised

4   black peppercorns, crushed

Method

Place the vinegar, tarragon and peppercorns in a crock with a cork or lid— a wide-necked, screw-topped bottle may be used. Cover the crock or bottle with a clean cover and store in a cool, dry place for 2 weeks, shaking the crock or bottle occasionally.

Strain the vinegar mixture into a jug. Discard the contents of the strainer. Carefully pour the tarragon vinegar into a warm, clean dry bottle. Cork the bottle and store until needed.

Rice Water-Chestnut Stuffing

(Makes about 10 cups of stuffing)

Ingredients

1   large onion, chopped
½   cup butter or vegetable oil
¼   cup parsley, chopped
1   cup halved green grapes
½   cup sherry or orange juice
2   cups cooked rice

2   teaspoons salt
2   8-ounce (227 mL) cans water chestnuts, rinsed in boiling water, drained and sliced
½   cup chopped pecans
½   cup chopped dried apricots

Method

Cook onion in butter or oil until tender. Combine with parsley, grapes, sherry, cooked rice, salt, water chestnuts, pecans and apricots. Stuff into an 8–10-pound turkey. Bake extra stuffing in shallow casserole with turkey during last 30 minutes of roasting time.

Spiced Jerusalem Artichoke Relish

Jerusalem artichokes, also known as sunchokes, are undeservedly one of the least appreciated vegetables. They are crisp and slightly bitter, but bland enough to absorb and enhance a wide variety of different flavors. (Serves 6)

Ingredients

1	pound (500 g) scrubbed and thinly sliced Jerusalem artichokes	½	cup lemon juice
		½	teaspoon dill seed
½	cup vegetable oil (corn, safflower, sunflower or other pure vegetable oil)	2	cloves garlic, chopped
		2	tablespoons chopped chives
		2	tablespoons chopped fresh dill

Method

Cover artichoke slices with water and boil in a stainless steel or enamel saucepan, covered, for about 5 minutes.

Drain off water, leaving the artichoke slices in the hot pot. Pour the oil and lemon juice over and add dill seed and garlic. Mix thoroughly and simmer for 10 minutes, stirring frequently. Sprinkle with chives and dill. Serve hot as a relish with sliced roast beef.

Mushroom Gravy

(Makes about 2½ cups)

Ingredients

1	bunch green onions, chopped	2	tablespoons flour
2	tablespoons drippings or vegetable oil	1½	cups chicken broth
¾	pound (375 g) fresh mushrooms, sliced		

Method

Sauté the onions in drippings until browned. Add mushrooms and sauté a few minutes more. Add flour and cook, stirring until browned. Add broth and heat to boiling. Reduce heat and simmer a few minutes.

GUEST RECIPES

This season we have had an exciting troupe of guests. Our regulars returned: Herbert Sonzogni, Neils Kjeldson, Bonnie Stern and Lucy Waverman; and new faces arrived from far and near: Carmen Jones from Houston, Jane Freiman from Chicago, Peter Kump, Lydie Marshall and Bert Greene from New York. It was a star-studded season in Studio 7!

I have included as many of our guests' recipes as space would permit. Where the recipe has been omitted, I have provided the address of the cooking school run by the guest or the publisher of the cookbook in which the particular recipe appears.

And, as always, bon appetit!

GUESTS

Herbert Sonzogni, Chef
Babsi's Restaurant
1731 Lakeshore Road West
Mississauga, Ontario L5J 1J4

Rosti

Chef Herbert Sonzogni prepares this Rosti at Babsi's Restaurant as a delicious accompaniment to Slivers of Veal, Zurich-Style (see p. 128). (Serves 4)

Ingredients

8	large potatoes	4	slices bacon, diced
3	tablespoons butter		Salt
1	onion, chopped		Pepper

Method

Bake or boil the potatoes in their skins. Drain, cool, peel and grate.

Heat a sauté pan, add butter, onion and bacon. Sauté until cooked. Add grated potatoes, salt and pepper. Sauté until golden brown on one side, turn, and sauté second side until brown. Cut into wedges and serve.

Quenelles of Pike
(Serves 4)

Ingredients

1	pound (500 g) pike, filleted and skinned		Salt to taste
1/4	cup unsalted butter, softened		White pepper to taste
1/2	cup dry white wine	8	cups fish stock*
4	eggs, separated	1	cup bechamel sauce
1/2	teaspoon dried marjoram leaves	1/2	cup 35% cream
1/4	teaspoon freshly grated nutmeg	1/2	cup hollandaise sauce

Method

Pass the pike through a fine grinder. Place in a food processor and with machine running, add the butter, wine, egg yolks, marjoram, nutmeg, salt and pepper through the feed tube. Blend until smooth. Beat the egg whites until stiff and fold into pike mixture.

Form the quenelles by scooping the mixture with two tablespoons, making almond-shaped forms.

Heat the fist stock to boiling. Poach the quenelles in stock for 10–12 minutes. Remove quenelles and drain well.

Heat the bechamel sauce. Stir in the cream. Reduce until sauce is thick enough to coat the quenelles. Remove from heat and fold in hollandaise sauce.

Place the quenelles in a buttered gratin dish. Coat with sauce. Broil just until golden brown, 1–2 minutes. Serve immediately.

Red Wine Vinegar Dressing
(Makes 1 1/3 cups)

Ingredients

1/3	cup red wine vinegar	Salt to taste
1	cup olive oil	Pepper to taste
1/4	teaspoon dry mustard	

---

*See *What's Cooking*, Volume 3, p. 67 for a recipe of fish stock. Also available at specialty fish stores.

Method

Whisk the vinegar into olive oil. Add mustard, salt and pepper. Whisk again to combine thoroughly.

Warm Salad of Romaine and Slivers of Beef Tenderloin

Serve this warm salad as a main-course lunch or dinner dish. The taste is exciting and the appearance colorful. (Serves 4)

Ingredients

1	bunch romaine lettuce	½	pound (300 g) beef tenderloin, cut into slivers
1	red pepper, cut into julienne strips		Salt to taste
1	cup red wine vinegar dressing (p. 126)		Pepper to taste
3	tablespoons olive oil	½	cup red wine

Method

Cut, wash and dry the romaine lettuce. Add the red pepper, dressing, and toss.

In a sauté pan, heat olive oil until it smokes. Add the tenderloin, salt and pepper. Sauté rare, then deglaze the pan with the red wine and pour over the salad. Serve immediately.

Warm Salad of Spinach and Scallops

What a delicious change for a summertime patio dinner! Just-cooked scallops served hot on a crisp bed of fresh spinach and red pepper. (Serves 4)

Ingredients

4	cups spinach leaves	½	cup white wine
1½	cups sliced mushrooms	½	pound (300 g) scallops
1	cup walnut oil dressing (p. 128)		Salt
			White pepper

Method

Remove stems from the spinach, wash and dry. Add the mushrooms and dressing, then toss.

In a sauté pan, preboil the white wine for 5 minutes to reduce. Add the scallops, salt and pepper. Simmer 2 minutes and then pour over the salad.

Slivers of Veal Zurich-Style
(Serves 4)

Ingredients

1 tablespoon butter or pure vegetable oil	1 cup sliced mushrooms
1 pound (500 g) veal, slivered	1/4 cup white wine
Salt to taste	1/4 cup thickened beef stock
Freshly ground pepper to taste	1/4 cup 35% cream
1 onion, chopped	1 tablespoon chopped parsley

Method

Heat sauté pan, add butter or oil. Sauté veal slivers, adding salt and pepper. Remove from pan. Add onion to sauté pan, then mushrooms. Deglaze pan with white wine, then add beef stock and cream. Reduce to the desired thickness. Return the veal slivers to pan for a moment. Sprinkle with parsley and rosti potatoes.

Walnut Oil Dressing
(Makes about 1½ cups)

Ingredients

1/4 cup walnut oil	Salt to taste
3/4 cup corn oil	Pepper to taste
1/2 cup white wine vinegar	1/2 teaspoon sugar

Method

Mix the walnut and corn oils. Whisk into vinegar. Season with salt, pepper and sugar.

Gary Brown, Chef
Southern Palms Beach Club
Barbados
West Indies

Barbadian Spiced Chicken
(Serves 4)

Ingredients

4	boneless chicken breasts	¼	teaspoon pepper
1	medium onion, chopped	½	cup flour
2	cloves garlic, chopped	1	egg mixed with 1 tablespoon milk
1	green onion, chopped		
1	teaspoon thyme	½	cup breadcrumbs
1	tablespoon chopped parsley	2	tablespoons butter
1	teaspoon Worcestershire sauce	2	tablespoons vegetable oil (corn, safflower, sunflower or other pure vegetable oil)
5	drops Tabasco sauce		
1	teaspoon salt		

Method

Pound the chicken breasts with a mallet until thin. Mix together the onion, garlic, green onion, thyme, parsley, Worcestershire sauce, Tabasco sauce, salt and pepper. Place one-quarter of this mixture on each chicken breast and roll up. Each breast may be held together with a toothpick, if desired. Dip the rolled chicken in flour, then in egg wash and finally in breadcrumbs. Heat butter and vegetable oil in a sauté pan. Fry in the hot butter-oil mixture 5 minutes per side, until golden brown. Place in a preheated 350°F (180°C) oven for 10 minutes to finish.

Barbadian-Style Bananas

Ingredients

2	bananas	1	teaspoon cinnamon
¼	cup dark rum	½	teaspoon ginger
¼	cup sugar syrup	1	tablespoon kirsch

Method

Peel and slice bananas. Mix all the remaining ingredients together and pour over bananas. Marinate in refrigerator for 1½ hours and serve.

Jean François Casari, Chef
King Edward Hotel,
37 King Street East,
Toronto, Ontario
M5C 1E7

Seafood Brochette with Tomato Sauce and Black Olive Purée
(Serves 2)

Ingredients

Tomato Sauce

1	medium onion, chopped	Pepper to taste
1	clove garlic, chopped	½ teaspoon dried thyme (or 1 stem fresh thyme, chopped)
2	tablespoons olive oil	
3	tomatoes, peeled, seeded and chopped	¼ cup chicken stock
2	teaspoons tomato paste	¼ teaspoon dried tarragon leaves (or 1 stem fresh tarragon, chopped)
½	teaspoon sugar	
	Salt to taste	

Method

Sauté the onion and garlic in olive oil until softened. Add tomatoes, tomato paste, sugar, salt, pepper, and thyme. Simmer 20 minutes. Add the chicken stock to thin sauce, if desired. Press sauce through a sieve or blend in blender. Stir in tarragon.

Ingredients

Olive Purée

1	teaspoon chopped shallots	1	cup black olives, pitted and sliced
1	tablespoon olive oil	½	cup fish stock

Method

Sauté shallots in olive oil until softened. Add olives and fish stock. Simmer 10 minutes. Purée in blender or food processor.

Ingredients

Brochettes

2	¼-pound (125 g) sole fillets	4	scallops
4	shrimp		

Method

Using bamboo skewers, make 2 brochettes with 1 sole fillet, 2 shrimp and 2 scallops on each one. Beginning with one end of the sole fillet, thread the skewer through, alternating shrimp and scallop pieces with the fillet so that the shrimp and scallops are positioned between folds of the sole. Broil or barbecue the brochettes until done, about 2 minutes per side, depending on the heat of the broiler or fire and distance from broiler or coals. Serve brochettes on a bed of tomato sauce, accompanied by black olive purée. Saffron rice would be a delicious accompaniment.

Lobster with Calvados Sauce and Apples
(Serves 2)

Ingredients

1	1½-pound (750 g) fresh, live lobster		2	tablespoons Calvados
3	cups water		2	cups fish stock
½	cup white wine		2	apples, peeled and sliced
2	tablespoons butter		1	cup 35% cream
1	carrot, peeled and diced		1	teaspoon melted butter
1	stalk celery, chopped			Salt to taste
1	medium onion, chopped			Pepper to taste
½	cup white wine			Fresh chervil or parsley for garnish

Method

Cut claws and tail from the lobster. Mix the water and ½ cup of white wine in a saucepan. Add lobster claws and tail and poach 10 minutes. Remove lobster from court bouillon, take meat from shell and reserve.

Sauté carrot, celery and onion in butter 5 minutes. Add the white wine, Calvados, fish stock, ½ the apple slices, cream and remaining body of lobster. Simmer all together 30 minutes. Sieve. Pick apple pieces out of the sieve, mash and add to sauce.

Brush the remaining sliced apple with melted butter and broil 2 minutes, until just golden brown.

Divide the sauce between 2 dinner plates. Place the reserved lobster meat on sauce and garnish with broiled apple slices and chervil or parsley.

Terry Seed, Chef
Hazelton Lanes Restaurant
Hazelton Lanes
Toronto, Ontario

Hazelton Cheesecake

Here is chef Terry Seed's rich, failure-proof cheesecake. He serves it with a purée of raspberries in sauce for an extra touch of color and taste. This is a special dessert and one that is sure to please. (Serves 12)

Ingredients

Graham Cracker Crust

1	cup Graham crumbs	2	tablespoons melted butter
1	tablespoon sugar		

Cheese Filling

1½	pounds (3 250 g packages) cream cheese—preferably fresh, not packaged cheese		Zest of 1 lemon
		6	eggs
1	cup sugar		Vanilla

Sour Cream Topping

1	cup sour cream	⅓	cup sugar

Raspberry Coulis

1	15-ounce (425 g) package frozen raspberries, thawed	1½	teaspoons cornstarch
2	tablespoons sugar	1	tablespoon kirsch

Method

Combine crumbs and sugar: mix well with melted butter and spread evenly over the surface of a 10-inch springform pan. Press crumbs smooth with your fingers. Combine cream cheese and sugar in a large mixer bowl and beat until well blended. Add zest of lemon, beaten eggs and vanilla. Beat, preferably with an electric mixer, for 10 minutes. Pour into springform pan. Bake at 300°F (150°C) for 1 hour. Rest in the oven for 10 minutes.

Add sour cream topping and bake 10 minutes more.

To make raspberry coulis drain the frozen raspberries in a sieve; reserve the liquid. Combine liquid with sugar in a small saucepan and bring to the boil. Add a bit of the hot liquid to the cornstarch to dissolve it; add it back into the saucepan and bring to the boil, stirring briskly with a whisk. Cook until the sauce thickens and remove from the heat. Cover and allow to cool. Meanwhile, push the raspberries through a sieve. When the cornstarch mixture is cooled, combine with sieved raspberries and kirsch. Pour into a pitcher and serve cold with cheesecake.

Terry Allen, Teaching Chef
George Brown College
P.O. 1015
Station B
Toronto, Ontario
M5T 2T9

Baked Bread Pudding

Young people flock to Teaching Master Terry Allen's cooking classes at George Brown College for recipes like this. (Serves 4)

Ingredients

6-8	slices buttered bread, without crusts	4	large eggs
2	tablespoons currants	⅓	cup sugar
1¼	cups milk	1	teaspoon vanilla

Method

Preheat oven to 375°F (190°C). Cut bread into quarters and arrange in a baking dish in layers, alternating the currants in between. Finish with a layer of buttered bread. Mix milk, eggs and sugar in a bowl, flavor with vanilla and beat until well mixed. Pour this over the bread and let soak for 15 minutes. Place the dish in a water bath, then in oven and bake about 30-40 minutes or until the custard is firm and the pudding puffs and is golden brown. Serve warm with warm butterscotch sauce (see following).

Butterscotch Sauce

This sauce is also delicious over ice cream or carrot pudding at Christmas.
(Makes 1½ cups)

Ingredients

⅓ cup soft brown sugar	2 tablespoons cornstarch
½ cup butter	¼ cup cold water
1 cup 35% cream	

Method

Place sugar and butter in a heavy saucepan and gently heat to melt together. Be careful not to burn.

Add the cream, stirring with a wooden spoon and gently reboil briefly. Mix cornstarch with cold water and add to mixture, stir and gently cook until sauce thickens. Serve warm over bread pudding.

Sauce will keep 2–3 weeks in the fridge.

Raffaello Ferrari, Chef
Pronto Ristorante
692 Mount Pleasant Road
Toronto, Ontario
M4S 2N3

Veal with Pistachio Nuts
(Serves 4)

Ingredients

½ cup blanched pistachio nuts	¾ cup 35% cream
¼ cup nut liqueur (Frangelico or Amaretto suggested)	1 teaspoon unsalted butter
	2 tablespoons white wine
2 pounds (1 kg) veal loin	Fresh parsley sprigs
2 tablespoons olive oil	2 tablespoons toasted sliced
2 tablespoons cognac	almonds

Method

Marinate pistachio nuts in liqueur for one hour. Slice the veal into ¼-inch slices. Heat oil in a large skillet and quickly sear veal on both sides. Drain pan and discard drippings. Flambé veal with cognac. Add the marinated pistachio nuts and cream. Cook slowly, over moderate heat until sauce is reduced by one-half. Remove veal slices and place on warm platter. Add butter and white wine to the sauce in the pan. Heat together 2 minutes. Pour sauce over the veal, garnish with parsley and toasted almonds.

Fettucine Natasha

(Serves 6)

Ingredients

1	tablespoon unsalted butter	¼	cup vodka
1	tablespoon olive oil	¾	cup 35% cream
2	shallots, chopped	1	pound (500 g) fresh spinach fettucine
1	clove garlic, chopped		
1	cup cubed smoked salmon	6	teaspoons black caviar
1	large tomato, cored, peeled and diced	⅔	cup freshly grated Parmesan cheese
	Salt to taste	1	tablespoon chopped parsley
	Pepper to taste		

Method

Heat the butter and oil together in a small saucepan or skillet. Sauté shallots and garlic until golden. Add the salmon, tomato, salt and pepper. Cook together for 2 minutes. Stir in vodka. Reduce heat and allow the mixture to simmer until liquid is reduced by half. Stir in cream and simmer again until volume is reduced by half.

Cook fettucine in boiling salted water until *al dente*. Drain and place on a warm serving platter. Add the sauce and toss to coat evenly. Sprinkle with caviar, cheese and parsley. Serve immediately.

Peter Kump's New York Cooking School
307 East 92nd Street
New York, New York
10125

Pastry Crust

Breadcrumbs can be made easily with your food processor from stale bread. If the breadcrumbs are too moist and absorbent, dry them out a bit in a 350°F (180°C) oven, but be careful not to burn them. If you are using fresh bread, put the slices whole into the oven before processing.

Ingredients

2	tablespoons unsalted butter	8-12	tablespoons freshly made breadcrumbs

Method

With your fingers, smear the butter very generously all around the bottom and sides of an 8, 9, or 10-inch pie or cake pan with a fixed bottom, or any baking dish suitable for presentation. If the butter is very soft, refrigerate for a few minutes before adding the breadcrumbs.

Sprinkle all the breadcrumbs over the butter and tilt the dish so that all the buttered surfaces are covered with crumbs. Press the crumbs into the butter with a fork, then knock out any excess by tapping the dish upside down. Refrigerate until ready to use.

Recipes courtesy of Peter Kump, *Quiche and Pâtés* (New York: Irena Chalmers)

Kren Quiche
(Beef with Horseradish)

Ingredients

1	9-inch prebaked quiche shell	6	ounces fresh or prepared horseradish
1½–2	cups cooked beef, cut in thin julienne strips	1	teaspoon salt
			Freshly ground pepper
1½	cups crème fraîche or heavy cream	2	tablespoons freshly minced parsley
3	large eggs		

Method

Preheat oven to 375°F (190°C). Place the beef strips in the quiche shell, covering the bottom. If you are using fresh horseradish, peel and coarsely grate it. In a bowl, mix the cream, eggs, horseradish (with the juices from the bottle if you are not using the fresh root), salt, pepper, and parsley. Pour the horseradish-cream mixture into the quiche shell and bake for 25–30 minutes, or until set and beginning to brown.

Parisian Brie Quiche

Ingredients

1	8-inch prebaked quiche shell	2	large eggs
4	ounces Brie, rind removed	1	tablespoon minced fresh chives
5	ounces fresh cream cheese		
2	tablespoons butter, at room temperature	1	teaspoon salt
			Freshly ground pepper
3	tablespoons heavy cream		

Method

Preheat oven to 375°F (190°C). Cream the cheeses with the butter in an electric mixer or in a food processor. Add the cream, eggs and chives to the cheese and butter and mix well.

Taste for seasoning and add salt and pepper to taste. Mix well. Pour the mixture into the shell and bake for 25–35 minutes, or until browned and set. Let cool 5 minutes before serving.

Jane Salzfass Freiman

Recipes are from *The Art of Food Processor Cooking*, Chicago: Contemporary Books, 1980.

Stuffed Pizza Dough
(Makes enough for one 14-inch stuffed pizza)

Ingredients

1	cup unbleached all-purpose flour or bread flour	1	cup cake and pastry flour
1¼	teaspoons dry active yeast	1½	teaspoons salt
1	cup warm water (110°F/45°C)	¼	cup olive oil or vegetable oil
2–2¼	cups unbleached all-purpose flour or bread flour*	⅓	cup warm water (110°F/45°C)

Method

Place the 1 cup of unbleached all-purpose flour or bread flour in a medium-sized bowl with the yeast. Stir in warm water until the mixture is thick and batterlike. Cover the bowl tightly with plastic. Set aside to rise until bubbly, thickened and approximately doubled in bulk—about 2–2½ hours.

Fit processor container with steel blade. Process the unbleached flour or bread flour, cake flour and salt with two 5-second pulses. With the machine running, pour olive oil and warm water through feed tube within 15 seconds. Continue processing, pouring starter through the feed tube as quickly as possible. When all the starter is added, process 30–40 seconds longer, until the dough forms a smooth ball that is the same consistency all the way through.

---

*Use the smaller amount if using Canadian flour. Add up to ¼ cup if the dough is too moist.

Rinse a large bowl with warm water; drain but do not dry. Add dough. Cover with plastic and set aside to rise until dough is slightly more than triple in bulk, approximately 2½ hours, depending on room temperature. When it has risen, dough is ready to press down, divide and roll for pizza. Keep the dough covered until ready to use. If desired, pressed-down dough may be returned to a bowl, covered, and refrigerated overnight or until ready to roll; it will rise again.

Chicago Stuffed Pizza
(Makes one 14-inch round double-crust pizza)

Ingredients

Filling

2	medium cloves garlic, peeled		2	medium onions, peeled, halved
3	tablespoons olive or vegetable oil			Salt
				Freshly ground pepper
4	790 g cans Italian plum tomatoes, drained, seeded, and juice reserved, or		1	pound (500 g) fresh mushrooms, wiped clean
6	pounds (2.7 kg) ripe tomatoes, peeled, seeded, halved		3	tablespoons olive or vegetable oil
1	teaspoon dried basil leaves		1	pound (500 g) sweet Italian sausage
1½	teaspoons dried oregano leaves		¾	teaspoon ground fennel seeds (optional)
2	tablespoons olive or vegetable oil		¾	pound (375 g) chilled Mozzarella cheese, cut into chunks
1	tablespoon butter			

Topping

2	tablespoons olive or vegetable oil		2	ounces Parmesan cheese, cut into chunks

Method

Prepare the dough (see p. 142) at least 4–5 hours in advance.

Insert steel blade in the food processor. With machine running, drop garlic cloves through feed tube and process until minched. Transfer garlic to a large skillet and add 3 tablespoons oil. Cook garlic over low heat until soft but not brown; set skillet aside. Change to the French-fry disk. Fill feed tube with tomatoes and process with a gentle push. Empty container as necessary into skillet and repeat until all tomatoes are cut into small pieces. Cook in skillet over medium heat until tomatoes are slightly thickened and nearly all the liquid has evaporated, about 40–45 minutes. Stir in basil and oregano leaves; remove to a bowl to cool.

Add 2 tablespoons oil and the butter to skillet; set aside. Change to the slicing disk. Slice onion halves with a gentle push; transfer to skillet and cook over medium heat until onions soften, about 10–15 minutes. Add salt and pepper to taste; set onions aside in a bowl.

Slice mushrooms with a gentle push. Heat 3 tablespoons oil in the same skillet; add mushrooms and sauté until dry. Season with salt and pepper and set aside in a bowl to cool.

Place bulk sausage in skillet or, if necessary, remove sausage from casings. Add fennel if desired. Cook over medium heat until sausage has turned pale in color and is thoroughly cooked; remove with slotted spoon and set aside.

Change processor disk to the shredding disk. Shred Mozzarella cheese with a gentle push; empty container into a bowl.

Remove dough from bowl without kneading. Divide into 2 portions, one equal to one-third of the total dough; the second equal to two-thirds.

To assemble the pizza, lightly flour a work surface. Roll out the larger ball of dough to a 20-inch circle. Place in an ungreased deep-dish pizza pan, letting the excess dough hang over sides. Brush the dough with 1 tablespoon oil and sprinkle lightly with salt. Spread 1 cup of Mozzarella cheese over dough. Scatter sausage pieces evenly over cheese. Distribute mushrooms over sausage, add onions and top with three-quarters of the tomato mixture, spread in an even layer. Top with 1⅓ cups Mozzarella cheese.

Brush the sides of the dough and overhanging part with water; set pan aside.

Roll out the remaining dough to a 14-inch circle. Place it over the filling and carefully stretch to touch and adhere to the bottom dough. Press all around to seal, trim bottom dough so that it hangs over the rim of the pan ½ inch. Brush overhang with water and fold inward onto top of pizza. Pinch to form a raised edge. Cut an X in the centre of the top dough to make a steam vent.

Using the metal knife blade, process the Parmesan cheese until powdery. Brush the top of the dough with the remaining tablespoon of oil. Spread with remaining tomato mixture and top with remaining Mozzarella and the Parmesan cheese. Brush the edge of the crust with cold water. (Pizza may now be refrigerated for 2 hours before baking, if desired.)

Adjust the oven rack to lower position. Heat oven to 450°F (230°C.) Bake until well browned and thoroughly hot, 30–40 minutes. Serve immediately from pan, first cutting into wedges. If no breaks occur in the bottom crust, pizza may also be removed from pan and placed on a board for serving.

Mini Pâtés

This pâté mixture can be baked in glazed earthenware onion soup bowls, without lids, as described here. The bowls are relatively inexpensive and make a great holiday gift when filled with Jane Freiman's homemade pâté. (Makes 6 pâtés, about 1¼ cups each)

Ingredients

½	cup minced onion	¼	teaspoon ground mace
1¼	teaspoons minced garlic	¼	teaspoon ground sage
3	tablespoons unsalted butter	⅛	teaspoon freshly ground pepper
4	ounces (125 g) skinned, boned chicken breast, diced into ¼-inch pieces	⅛	teaspoon ground cloves
		⅛	teaspoon cardamom
4	ounces (125 g) boiled ham, diced into ¼-inch pieces	⅛	teaspoon cinnamon
		1½	pounds (750 g) fresh pork fatback, cut into ½-inch thick sheets, chilled
1½	tablespoons cognac or brandy		
1	pound (500 g) ground veal	6	imported bay leaves
1	pound (500 g) ground pork	6	teaspoons dried thyme
½	pound (250 g) coarsely ground fresh pork fat	3	tablespoons whole black peppercorns
2	large eggs, lightly beaten	3	tablespoons whole white peppercorns
2	teaspoons salt		
½	teaspoon dried marjoram	1	teaspoon crushed red pepper flakes
½	teaspoon dried basil		
¼	teaspoon ground allspice		

Method

Sauté the onion and garlic in two tablespoons of the butter, until soft, about 3 minutes. Transfer with a slotted spoon to a small bowl, then chill. Add the remaining butter and chicken to the same pan and toss over high heat until the chicken is opaque, about 3 minutes. Add the ham and toss to coat. Remove from the heat and add the cognac; ignite and shake the pan until the flames subside. Cool, then chill.

Combine the cooked onion, veal, pork, ground fat, eggs, salt and the spices, from marjoram to cinnamon inclusive, in a large bowl. Mix thoroughly. Sauté a tablespoon of this mixture, taste it, and adjust the seasonings to be slightly spicy, as the flavors will be dulled by chilling and mellowed by aging. Stir the chicken and ham mixture into the seasoned ground meat.

Line 6 onion soup crocks with fatback sheets so that the bottoms and sides are covered and there is enough overlap to cover the top of the meat completely. Pack the meat firmly into the crocks. Fold the fatback over the tops. Rap several times on the counter to remove air pockets. Press 1 bay leaf, 1 teaspoon thyme, 1 tablespoon mixed black and white peppercorns and a sprinkling of red pepper flakes onto the fatback in each bowl and make a couple of ½-inch slits in the top.

Place the crocks in a roasting pan and pour in hot tap water to come halfway up the sides of the bowls. Bake in a preheated 325°F (160°C) oven until an instant-read thermometer inserted in the middle of the pâté registers 165°F (72°C), about 2¼ hours.

Let cool in the water for 10 minutes. Then remove the crocks from the water and cool completely on wire racks.

Wipe the crock bottoms with a hot wet rag to remove any traces of fat. Refrigerate 3 days before serving, or up to 2 weeks.

From *Gifts From the Christmas Kitchen* New York; Irena Chalmers Cookbooks, 1983.

Fresh Fruit Tart
(Serves 8)

Pastry Cream

Ingredients

1 cup heavy cream	3 tablespoons all-purpose flour
¼ cup sugar	½ teaspoon vanilla
3 egg yolks	½ teaspoon unsalted butter, cut
Pinch of salt	into tiny pieces

Method

Combine ¾ cup of the cream with sugar in a small heavy saucepan. Heat over low heat, stirring to dissolve the sugar. Remove from heat.

Whisk egg yolks and salt in a heavy, medium saucepan. Whisk in the ¼ cup unheated cream. Whisk in flour until smooth. Slowly pour in the hot cream mixture, whisking vigorously.

Place the saucepan over low heat. Whisk vigorously until the mixture thickens to consistency of a thick pudding, about 5 minutes. Do not allow to simmer. Whisk in vanilla, then transfer pastry cream to bowl. Dot top of cream with butter. Cover with plastic wrap applied directly to surface. Let cool at room temperature.

When the pastry cream is cool, thoroughly stir in any butter left on surface. Cover again. Refrigerate until thoroughly chilled.

Tart Shell

Ingredients

1	egg	2	teaspoons sugar
1	teaspoon fresh lemon juice	½	cup unsalted butter
	Pinch of salt		
1¼	cups unbleached all-purpose flour		

Method

Combine the egg, lemon juice and salt in a small bowl. Beat well with fork.

Combine the flour and sugar in a large bowl. Cut in butter until mixture is pale yellow and has the texture of coarse sand. Stir in egg mixture. Mix to form a soft dough. Turn the dough out onto a large sheet of plastic wrap. Flatten the dough into a rectangle about 8 inches × 4 inches. Refrigerate dough, wrapped in plastic, until firm—about 1 hour.

Roll out the chilled dough between two pieces of waxed paper to a rectangle about 17 inches × 7 inches. Cutting through the paper, trim dough to a 16 inch × 5 inch rectangle. Peel off top sheet of waxed paper; invert pastry rectangle onto a wet baking sheet. Peel away remaining paper. From trimmings, using ruler as a guide, cut 2 long strips, each 16 inches long and ¼ inch wide, and 2 shorter strips, each 5 inches long and ¼ inch wide.

Using a pastry brush dipped in cold water, moisten edges of pastry rectangle on all sides. Place each pastry strip on a corresponding edge of pastry; press strips gently to make them adhere to the base, then pinch gently at ends to form a continuous raised edge. Pierce pastry base with skewer or fork at 2-inch intervals. Refrigerate, on baking sheet, 15 minutes.

Adjust oven rack to lowest position. Heat oven to 375°F (190°C).

Bake tart shell until pale golden, 15–18 minutes. Cool thoroughly on baking sheet.

Bake 375° 5 min   9" tart pan

1½ c all purpose flour
½ c cake + pastry flours
3/4 c unsalted butter well chilled cut in cubes
Pinch of salt
1 - 2 T ice water (depends on how cold butter is)
2 egg yolks or plus 2 hard cooked egg yolks
Variation:
+ sugar + lemon rind - nice for lemon filling
+ wine instead of water
No need to use rolling pin - Press dough into pan.

Filling

Ingredients

3 tablespoons strained apricot or raspberry jam, or red currant jelly

½ teaspoon kirsch or cognac

⅓ cup leftover cake crumbs (from pound or sponge cake) or ¼ cup fresh breadcrumbs

1 pint large strawberries, hulled, stem ends cut flat

½ small pineapple, pared, cored, quartered, cut into ⅛-inch slices

2 medium kiwis, peeled, cut into ⅛-inch slices

8 ounces (250 g) large black grapes, stem ends cut flat, seeded

1 medium papaya, pared, halved, seeded, cut into ⅛-inch slices

Icing sugar (optional)

Method

Stir jam and kirsch together in a small, heavy saucepan over low heat, just until the jam is melted and warmed through. Remove from heat.

Place cooled tart shell on a serving board or platter, handling the brittle pastry gently. Brush warm jam over the surface of the pastry, excluding rim. Sprinkle evenly with cake crumbs while the jam is still warm. Let stand 5 minutes.

Smooth dollops of pastry cream over crumbs at even intervals. Using a small icing spatula, spread the cream in a thin layer, covering pastry base completely and evenly. Remove any excess cream from outside rim, wiping carefully with paper towel.

Place fruit over pastry cream in lengthwise rows, working from left to right. Place strawberries, hulled ends down, against one long edge so they do not extend beyond the rim. Place pineapple slices, closely overlapping, against the berries. Arrange kiwi slices, overlapping, next to the pineapple. Place grapes, stem ends down, along outside edge of tart so they do not extend beyond rim. Fit papaya slices, in groups of 3, between kiwis and grapes, trimming them to fit if necessary.

Cover the tart loosely with plastic wrap. Refrigerate at least 1 hour and no longer than 6 to avoid discoloration of fruit. If desired, dust tart lightly with icing sugar just before serving.

Lydie Marshall
A La Bonne Cocotte
28 8th Avenue
New York, New York
10014

Parmesan Mousselines with Braised Asparagus Tips

Greenwich Village, New York, is home and school for cooking teacher Lydie Marshall. She stopped by our kitchen on the way to France. Crew and staff stood by enthralled while Lydie whipped together this elegant first course of individual cheese soufflés with cream sauce. (Serves 6)

Ingredients

1	pound (500 g) asparagus, cleaned, tips removed (reserve stalks for soup)
2	tablespoons butter
1	cup milk
⅓	cup flour
4	tablespoons unsalted butter

1	cup freshly grated Parmesan
3	egg yolks
2	egg whites
1	cup heavy cream
	Salt
	Pepper

Method

Preheat oven to 325°F (160°C). Steam the asparagus tips, then braise with 2 tablespoons butter. Season.

Heat the milk to warm. Pour it slowly into the flour and mix thoroughly. Whisk the mixture over medium-high heat until it thickens. Off the flame, add 4 tablespoons butter, one at a time, then add ½ cup freshly grated Parmesan, egg yolks, salt and pepper. Beat the 2 egg whites stiff. Fold into the mixture. Add the asparagus tips.

Brush butter on 6 individual moulds or ramekins. Fill each mould about ¾ full. Place in a water-bath about half way up the moulds. Bake in the middle shelf of the oven for about 20 minutes or until the top of the mousseline is spongy.

This dish may be prepared ahead of time up to this step. Unmould each soufflé into a greased gratin dish, **pour cream overtop** and add the rest of the grated Parmesan. Bake for another 15 minutes, or until the mousselines are puffy. Serve.

Carmen Jones
Carmen's Cuisine
6711 Seaton Valley
Spring, Texas
27373
U.S.A.

Guacamole

Carmen Jones suggests buying firm avocados and allowing them to ripen at home, using a method that could be called the "plunge in the flour bin." Place the avocados in a paper bag filled with flour and close the bag tightly. Leave until the avocados are just soft to the touch—usually 1–2 days. Having read this far, you are no doubt dying to know the principle behind this method. The flour holds the gases emitted by the ripening fruit close around it, thus hurrying the process. Trust me, it works! (Serves 6 as appetizer, 4 as salad)

Ingredients

2	large ripe avocados	½	teaspoon garlic salt
2	tablespoons finely chopped onion	1	tablespoon lemon juice
2	tablespoons finely chopped canned green chilies	2	tablespoons finely chopped tomato
			Additional lemon juice

Method

Cut the avocados in half and remove pits. Spoon soft avocado out of the shells into a mixing bowl. Mix well to form a chunky paste. Add all the remaining ingredients except the tomato and additional lemon juice. Mix well. Season to taste. Spoon into a serving bowl and garnish with chopped tomato and sprinkle lightly with additional lemon juice to prevent the mixture from darkening. Serve with tortilla chips.

Quesadillas
(Serves 8)

Ingredients

8	corn tortillas (uncrisped, flat)	1	can whole green chilies
	Strips of Monterrey Jack or Mozzarella cheese	3	cups vegetable oil for deep frying

Method

Place strips of cheese and green chilies in the centre of each tortilla. Fold over as a turnover and pinch the edges securely together. Hold them together between the tines of a fork, using the fork as a handle while deep frying.

Heat vegetable oil in deep fat fryer or wok. Fry each tortilla until slightly crisp, 30 seconds to 1 minute. Drain tortillas on absorbent paper towel and sprinkle with salt. Serve hot as an hors d'oeuvre or accompaniment with other Mexican food.

Tex-Mex Picadillo

Houston cooking teacher Carmen Jones says picadillo may be used to stuff peppers, tomato cups and onion cups.

Ingredients

1½	pounds (750 g) ground lean beef	⅓	cup vinegar
½	pound (250 g) coarsely ground pork	1	tablespoon sugar
1	large onion, finely chopped	2	teaspoons cinnamon
¼	cup vegetable oil (corn, safflower, sunflower or other pure vegetable oil)		Pinch ground cloves
		1	teaspoon ground cumin
			Salt and pepper to taste
1	large tomato, peeled, seeded and chopped	¾	cup seedless raisins
		1	cup blanched, slivered almonds
2	cloves garlic, mashed	1	cup drained stuffed green olives

Method

Brown the ground meat and onion in oil. Add tomato, garlic, vinegar, sugar and spices. Mix well. Season to taste with salt and pepper. Add raisins and cook gently for 30 minutes. Add blanched almonds and stuffed green olives. Heat thoroughly and serve with tortilla chips or crackers while warm.

Bunuelos

These crisp, paper-thin, deep-fried cookies are from Mexico by way of Texas. Remarkably like French beignets and Italian farfalette dolci, they are delicious sprinkled with cinnamon and heaps of sieved icing sugar. (Makes about 30)

Ingredients

3	tablespoons anise seed	1	teaspoon salt
1½–1¾	cups hot water	1	teaspoon baking powder
½	cup shortening (or half butter, half shortening)		Deep fat for frying
4	cups flour		Ground cinnamon
			Granulated sugar

Method

Combine the hot water and anise seed and let steep over low heat for 20 minutes. Strain out seeds.Cut shortening into the flour, salt and baking powder. Add in hot anise tea and stir into a ball. Add only enough water to make a medium dough. Turn out and knead for 15 minutes or use dough hook and knead for 5 minutes. Turn out and let rest for 20 minutes.

Separate into egg-sized balls and roll out on floured board until very thin. Let rest after rolling. Stretch with hands to increase size. Fry in deep fat until light golden brown turning once—30 seconds to 1 minute approximately. Drain on absorbent paper towel and sprinkle generously with a mixture of cinnamon and sugar.

Bonnie Stern
Bonnie Stern School of Cooking
6 Erskine Avenue
Toronto, Ontario
M4P 1Y2

Leg of Lamb with Rosemary and Garlic Sauce

Bonnie Stern developed this recipe from one demonstrated by Master Chef, Jacques Pepin. The flavor and aroma are superb—the taste is unforgettable. (Serves 6)

Ingredients

1	5-7 pound (2-3 kg) leg of lamb	1	cup dry white wine
1	cup diced onions	½	teaspoon dried rosemary
30	cloves garlic, unpeeled	6	cups water
1	28-ounce (796 mL) can plum tomatoes		Salt and pepper to taste
		2	tablespoons unsalted butter

Method

Trim most of the top fat from the lamb. Bone out and flatten the meat, removing any large pieces of fat from inside. Discard the fat. If possible, break the bones into smaller pieces. In a large saucepan brown the bones and any trimmed meat well. Add onions and cook 5 minutes. Add garlic, tomatoes, wine, rosemary and water. Bring to a boil and cook gently for 1 hour. Skim off any fat that rises to the surface.

Remove the bones and pass the sauce through a food mill. Boil vigorously to reduce liquid to 3 cups. Add salt and pepper to taste.

Melt the butter in a large roasting pan. Brown meat, fat side first on medium-high heat. Turn and brown meat 5 minutes more on second side. Place the lamb in a preheated 425°F (210°C) oven for 15 minutes. Let rest at 160°F (80°C) for 20 minutes before carving.

Deglaze pan with some sauce and stir to melt all the solidified juices on the bottom. Carve the roast into thin slices and serve with sauce around the meat or separately.

McCall's School of Cake Decorating
3810 Bloor Street West
Toronto, Ontario
M9B 6C2

Petits Fours

Here is the recipe for those rich and tiny fondant-covered cakes, demonstrated by Chef Willy Kristansen of the McCall's School of Cake Decorating in Toronto. (Makes 3 dozen)

Pastry

Ingredients

½	cup unsalted butter (room temperature)	1	teaspoon vanilla
¾	cup icing sugar	1¾	cups pastry flour
1	egg	½	cup raspberry or strawberry jam

Method

Cream the butter, gradually add icing sugar, and cream together. Beat in egg and vanilla. Fold in flour. (Do not overmix.) Cool dough before rolling it out.

Roll dough and cut to fit moulds or small tart shells. Place ½ teaspoon of jam in the bottom of each mould or shell, on top of pastry.

Almond Paste Filling

Ingredients

½ cup almond paste
2 eggs
⅓ cup unsalted butter (room temperature)

⅓ cup sugar
1 tablespoon all-purpose flour

Method

Soften the almond paste by slowly beating in eggs. Add butter, sugar and flour and mix until smooth. Put mixture in piping bag with wide nozzle. Pipe into shells. Bake at 350°F (180°C) 15-20 minutes until golden brown.

Butter Cream Filling

Ingredients

½ pound unsalted butter (room temperature)
1 cup custard

1-2 tablespoons liqueur, if desired
Food coloring, if desired

Method

Thoroughly cream butter. Blend in cooled custard, liqueur and food coloring. Spoon into a piping bag. Pipe a circle of butter cream on top of the almond paste in each shell. Chill.

Fondant

Ingredients

1 pound (500 g) package fondant (available in cake specialty stores)

Simple sugar syrup (equal parts sugar and water)
Food coloring, if desired

Method

Heat fondant in the top of a double boiler over gently boiling water. Gradually beat in syrup until fondant is desired thickness to spread. Add food coloring, if desired. Cool fondant slightly. Spoon into a piping bag. Pipe on petits fours using small nozzle. Fondant will run down sides and cover completely. Allow to set. Garnish with rosettes or candied violets.

Sachertorte

If you've ever wondered about the origins of sachertorte the answer is very simple. This fantastic chocolate torte owes its name to Frau Sacher, a noted personality in Vienna—in the days when Austria still enjoyed the spectacle of a ruling class but not the benefit of nobility paying its own way. Today, Frau Sacher's torte is sure to please all classes of taste.

Cake

Ingredients

9	tablespoons butter		8	egg whites
½	cup sugar		½	cup sugar
5	tablespoons cocoa		1	cup cake flour
1	teaspoon vanilla		1	cup ground hazelnuts
8	egg yolks			

Method

Cream butter and gradually beat in sugar, cocoa and vanilla. Beat in the egg yolks and cream all together. Beat egg whites until frothy. Gradually beat in sugar and whip until stiff. Fold the egg whites into yolk mixture. Combine flour and nuts and fold into batter. Pour batter into 2 greased and floured 8-inch round pans. Bake at 350°F (180°C), 35–40 minutes. Cool on rack. Remove from pans.

Topping and Glaze

Ingredients

½	cup apricot jam		1	cup whipping cream
½	pound (250 g) marzipan		8	ounces pure dark chocolate

Method

Heat the apricot jam. Roll marzipan to form 2 8-inch circles. Brush the jam on top of each layer and then place one layer on top of the other.

Boil cream for 2 minutes. Add chocolate, broken into pieces. Stir until dissolved. Cool. Pour chocolate-cream over the top of the cake. It will run down the sides to cover cake completely. Decorate top of the cake, if desired, after chocolate has set.

Irena Chalmers Cookbooks Inc.
23 East 92nd Street
New York, New York
10028

Pepper Jelly

A piquant but more refined version of the ubiquitous southern pepper sauce, this jelly can be spread on crackers and cream cheese, and is excellent with ham or with green beans or peas. (Makes 4 pints)

Ingredients

½ cup seeded and coarsely chopped hot red pepper

½ cup seeded and coarsely chopped hot green pepper

1 medium-sized onion, quartered

1½ cups vinegar

5½ cups sugar

1 bottle liquid pectin

Method

Process the peppers, onion and vinegar in a food processor until very finely chopped. Pour the sugar into a 6-quart pot. Add the chopped vegetables to the pot and let it come to a boil. Boil for 1 minute. Remove from the heat and stir in the pectin, skimming the foam for 5 minutes. Ladle the mixture into hot sterilized jars. Shake the jars to keep the peppers mixed. Let cool.

Pasta with Peas

Fresh peas are a glory of the Italian spring; they find their way into many dishes, including pasta. So do other vegetables in their seasons from asparagus to zucchini. The vegetable is usually cooked separately—either browned in oil, or boiled and then turned in butter—before being added to the basic sauce. (Serves 4-6)

Ingredients

1	pound spaghettini, linguini, tagliatelle, or fettucine	2	medium-sized tomatoes, peeled, seeded and chopped, or 1 cup canned Italian plum tomatoes, drained and chopped
1/4	cup olive oil		
1/4	pound prosciutto or other ham, chopped	1	tablespoon chopped fresh basil or 1 teaspoon dried
1	onion, chopped	1/2	teaspoon salt
1	garlic clove, minced		Freshly ground black pepper
1/2	cup finely chopped parsley	2	tablespoons butter
1/2	cup chicken broth	1	cup grated Parmesan cheese
1-2	cups fresh or frozen peas, par-boiled		

Method

Set 6 quarts of water to boil with 2 tablespoons of salt; this may take half an hour. Add the pasta and cook for 7 or 8 minutes, until tender but firm.

In a large enamelware skillet, heat the oil and add the ham, onion, garlic and parsley. Cook until the onion is soft. Add the broth and the peas, which have been partially cooked but should still be quite firm. Cook until the peas are almost done, then add the tomatoes and basil, salt and pepper to taste, and cook 2-3 minutes longer.

Drain the pasta and turn into a warm bowl. Add the sauce and the butter, and half the cheese. Toss gently and serve at once with the remaining cheese on the side.

Roasted Spiced Pecans

(Makes 4 cups)

Ingredients

2	teaspoons cinnamon	1	teaspoon sugar
1	teaspoon nutmeg	8	tablespoons butter, melted
1	teaspoon powdered ginger	1	pound (500 g) pecan halves
1	teaspoon salt		

Method

Preheat oven to 275°F (100°C). Combine the spices, salt and sugar in a bowl and stir half the mixture into the melted butter. Toss the nuts with the spiced butter, remove and place them in the oven to roast for 10–15 minutes, until nicely browned.

Remove the nuts from the oven and toss them with the remaining spice mixture. Spread them out on paper towels to drain and cool completely. Pack into pretty glass jars.

Apple Sage Vinegar

This vinegar is splendid for such dishes as red cabbage and apples or hot bacon dressings. (Makes 1 quart vinegar)

Ingredients

1	quart apple cider vinegar, 6 per cent acidity		1	medium-sized red tart apple, McIntosh or Winesap preferred
¼	cup sugar			
4	large sprigs fresh sage, washed, dried and left on stems (about 20 leaves)		1	bamboo skewer to fit inside bottle

Method

Combine the cider vinegar and the sugar in a non-aluminum saucepan. Bring to a simmer, stirring to dissolve the sugar. Simmer 1 minute.

Wash the label off the vinegar bottle and clean the bottle and cap thoroughly. Push the sage sprigs into the bottle. Remove the apple peel in a continuous strip and thread it onto the skewer. Place the skewer in the bottle.

Use a funnel to pour the warm vinegar into the bottle. Allow to cool to room temperature and then replace the cap. Store in a cool, dark place for at least 48 hours before using. The vinegar may be kept for up to 6 months.

Marinated Mushrooms

Throughout the year, collect attractive glass jars—any size or shape. Just before Christmas, fill them with small white mushrooms and cover with a vinaigrette. These make lovely, little gifts.

Ingredients

6	tablespoons fruity olive oil	½	teaspoon sugar
2	tablespoons red wine vinegar	1	teaspoon finely chopped garlic
1	teaspoon salt	1	tablespoon parsley
½	teaspoon freshly ground pepper	1	tablespoon freshly snipped chives
1	teaspoon Dijon mustard		Sprig fresh thyme, optional

Method

Combine all the ingredients in a food processor and blend. Add a sprig of fresh thyme to each jar, if you have it. Seal and store in a cool place.

Pickled Herring

(Serves 4-6)

Ingredients

2¼	cups water	2	whole cloves
1	cup white distilled vinegar, 5 per cent acidity	4	salt herring fillets, about 3 ounces each, skinned and desalted by soaking in several changes of water for 6 hours
½	cup beet juice		
⅔	cup sugar		
4	bay leaves	3	sprigs dill
¼	teaspoon white peppercorns, crushed	¼	small onion, sliced
		1	small carrot, julienned
25	allspice berries, coarsely chopped	½	stalk celery, diced

Method

Bring the water, vinegar, beet juice, sugar, bay leaves, pepper, allspice and cloves to a boil in a non-aluminum pan. Remove from the heat and let cool.

Cut the herring fillets diagonally into 1-inch pieces, keeping the shape of the fillets. Pour the pickling solution over the herring and stir in the dill, onion, carrot and celery. Let the herring marinate overnight in the refrigerator before eating.

Elizabeth Baird

Author of *Elizabeth Baird's 150 Favorites, Summer Berries, Apples, Peaches and Pears, Classic Canadian Cooking*. Published by James Lorimer & Co.

Marinated Three Pepper Salad
(Serves 6)

Ingredients

1	large head romaine lettuce	4-6	banana peppers, hot if desired
3	large red peppers		
3	large green peppers		

Dressing

2/3	cup olive oil	1/4	teaspoon paprika
3	tablespoons red wine vinegar	1/4	teaspoon coriander
1	teaspoon salt	1	large clove garlic
1/4	teaspoon freshly ground pepper	2	tablespoons finely chopped onion

Method

Wash lettuce and dry thoroughly. Keep chilled until time to arrange the salad.

Broil peppers, steam and peel. Cut into lengthwise strips, about 1/2 inch wide.

Combine all ingredients for the dressing. Marinate peppers in dressing for an hour or two, or longer if convenient. Keep chilled if preparing a day in advance, but bring back to room temperature before arranging.

Line a flat salad bowl with romaine leaves and fill attractively with peppers, keeping colors separate if desired. Pour dressing over.

The following guests have appeared on our show, although their recipes do not appear in this book. They can be reached for further information at the addresses provided.

Allergy Information Association,
Room #7
25 Poynter Drive
Weston, Ontario M9R 1K8

The Allergy Cookbook, Allergy Information Association, Methuen, 1983.

Werner Bassen, Chef
Fenton's Restaurant
2 Gloucester Street
Toronto, Ontario M4Y 1L5

Giuliano Buglialli
18 East 81st Street
New York, New York 10028

Author of *The Fine Art of Italian Cooking,* Times Books, 1979
        Classic Techniques of Italian Cooking, Simon and Schuster, 1982
        Foods of Italy, General Publishing, 1984

Beverly Burge
Beverly Burge School of Cooking
208 Berkeley Street
Toronto, Ontario M5A 2X4

Bert Greene,
240 West 12th Street
New York, New York 10014

Author of *Greene on Greens,* Workman Press, 1984

International Association of Cooking Schools
1001 Connecticut Avenue N.W.
Suite 800
Washington D.C. 20036

Hazel Maw
La Cuisine Imperiale Restaurant
36A Prince Arthur Avenue
Toronto, Ontario M5R 1B4

Lucy Waverman
The Cooking School
204 Glenayr Road
Toronto, Ontario M5P 3C3

EQUIPMENT USED ON WHAT'S COOKING
Available from Eaton's of Canada

The Compleat Kitchen
87 Yorkville Avenue
Toronto, Ontario
M5R 1C1

Embros Sales Limited
1170 Yonge Street
Toronto, Ontario
M4W 2L9

INDEX

Printed in Canada